The Reada

1 Chronicles
2 Chronicles

From Iron Stream Media

The Readable Bible is available as a complete Bible, in portions, in individual books as below, and as a twenty-seven-volume set.

Visit www.ironstreammedia.com for more information.

The Readable Bible

1 Chronicles
2 Chronicles

The Religious Practices of the Leaders

Translated and Edited by
Rodney S. Laughlin
Brendan I. Kennedy, PhD

IRON
STREAM

Birmingham, Alabama

The Readable Bible: 1 and 2 Chronicles

Iron Stream
An imprint of Iron Stream Media
100 Missionary Ridge
Birmingham, AL 35242
www.ironstreammedia.com

Library of Congress Control Number: 2022938636

Cover design: twoline || Studio

Interior designer/illustrator: Clyde Adams (www.clydeadams.com)

Map geographic features courtesy of Bible Mapper (www.biblemapper.com).

Typeface: Veritas AE from Altered Ego Fonts, a division of Aespire

2 3 4 5—26 25 24 23

Contents

1 Chronicles

Maps, tables, and charts are in italics

Part 1. Genealogies

Part 2. David's Reign

1 Chronicles 23

1 Chronicles 24

1 Chronicles 25

1 Chronicles 26

1 Chronicles 27

1 Chronicles 28

1 Chronicles 29

2 Chronicles

Part 1. Solomon's Reign

Part 2. The Divided Kingdom

Preface

To the Reader

One day I was standing in an airport bookstore looking for a book to read. I asked myself, "Why am I looking for something to read when I have a Bible in my briefcase?" I answered, "The Bible is hard to read. I want to read something easier." Then I asked myself, "Why is it so hard to read? You're a seminary graduate, a former pastor, a Bible teacher!" Thus began a quest that has led to The Readable Bible—the Bible as it would look if Moses, Joshua, Matthew, Mark, Paul, and the other writers had been sitting in front of a computer when God spoke through them.

It seems to me that the Bible is hard to read because all material is presented in sentence format. Today we use tables to present census information and charts for genealogies. When we want something built, we draw up a specification document. Law codes are organized in outline form. We use bullet points, bold text, and other aids to help us grasp information. Yet in today's Bibles, all the information is still presented in sentence format in plain text. Surely those men of old would have used modern formats if they had known about them when God spoke through them. Modern formatting does not change the information; it simply presents it in a way that makes it easier to grasp. The Readable Bible brings you the biblical text in modern formats.

You may struggle with the idea of Scripture in modern formats. Actually, all of today's Bibles present the text in a form much different from that of the original manuscripts. Consider how many format changes that were developed over the past two thousand years led to the format considered normal today. Each change was radical in its time:

- Vowels: The earliest Hebrew manuscripts have no vowels; they were added hundreds of years later.
- Capital Letters: The Hebrew Old Testament and the Greek New Testament manuscripts have no uppercase and lowercase letters.
- Punctuation: The original manuscripts have no punctuation (no commas or periods!).
- Chapter Numbers: These were not common in Bibles until the thirteenth century AD.
- Verse Numbers: The first verse-numbering system was developed over a thousand years after the last Bible book was written. It had one-third of today's verse numbers, making verses three or four times longer. Today's Christian Bible numbering system was not developed until the sixteenth century.
- Paragraphs: The first paragraphed King James Bible was published in the mid-1800s.

So presenting the words of Scripture in tables, cascading the text of long, complex sentences, and using other modern formatting techniques is simply continuing the long-term trend of making the Bible easier to understand.

Our hope is that people who have never read the Bible will decide to read this version because it is so approachable. Please give a copy to someone who struggles to understand the Bible and, especially, to those who do not read the Bible.

Acknowledgments

My thanks to all the members of our editing team, our volunteer development team, and the many others who have donated funds and worked to bring The Readable Bible to completion.

A big "thank you" to my designer and partner in this project, Clyde Adams, for joining me in this faith venture. He has turned the translation into well-laid-out text and my formatting concepts into reality. The maps, tables, charts, and book layout are all his work.

Most of all, I thank my wife, Rebecca, for her ideas, her love, and her strong support of this endeavor over the past twelve years.

Dedication

And now I dedicate to our Lord this translation of his holy Word, humbly asking him to grant that it may bring forth fruit to his glory and the building up of his people.

Rodney A. Laughlin

Spring 2022

Introduction to Chronicles

When two or more people write the story of their life in their homeland, the reports are never the same. Each writer experiences the event in their own personal way, sees its significance from their perspective, and has their own purpose for writing the history. Thus, while the four books of 1 and 2 Samuel and 1 and 2 Kings are written about the same period as 1 and 2 Chronicles, they differ in emphasis. The former focus on political and military events, and they feature prophets and kings as the main characters. Chronicles (originally one book, later divided into two) focuses on the religious practices of the kings, priests, and Levites. It features the kings of Judah as the main characters, mostly omitting the prophets who are so prominent in Samuel and Kings. While many of the same events and persons are covered, they are not presented in the same fashion or for the same purpose.

All the historical books (Samuel, Chronicles, and Kings, six books in all) present a theological history of Israel. Each shows that God requires obedience, and that disobedience can have dire consequences—in this case, the dividing of the strong nation of Israel into two weak nations, Judah in the south and Israel in the north.[a]

Samuel and Kings show us how the unfaithfulness of the kings led to the destruction of Israel and Judah and the deportation of the Israelites into Assyria and Babylonia. Chronicles emphasizes religion and worship according to the Law as the glue that God uses to hold his people together. And it shows how even irregular but sincere worship, and especially repentance by a king, sometimes leads to God's pleasure and to his judgment being delayed or averted.

Second Kings ends on a pessimistic note, with Israel totally defeated and wiped out, Judah in exile, and no clue as to who will lead Judah or how any Israelites will survive as God's people. Chronicles ends on an optimistic note, with King Cyrus of Persia giving permission for Jews to return to the promised land and rebuild the temple. According to Chronicles, the real Israel—God's faithful, worshiping community—will go on.

Before You Read

Words in *italics* are additions to the biblical text. In the context of commands, rules, and regulations, "shall," "must," and "are/is to" are equal terms, all the same strength.

Read lists from top to bottom in the first column then read the next column.

You will find a "Key to Genealogical Tables" in the back of the book. While we have endeavored to make our tables intuitive, you may grasp them more quickly if you look at the key first.

We encourage you to read "Translation Notes" and "Format and Presentation Notes" in the back of the book. They are easy reading and will increase your understanding of the text.

Please browse the glossary before you begin reading. You will find helpful information about words that appear frequently in this book, as well as important explanations of the words "Lord" and "Yahweh."

---

a   After the split, Israel is referred to as *"Northern* Israel" in The Readable Bible historical books.

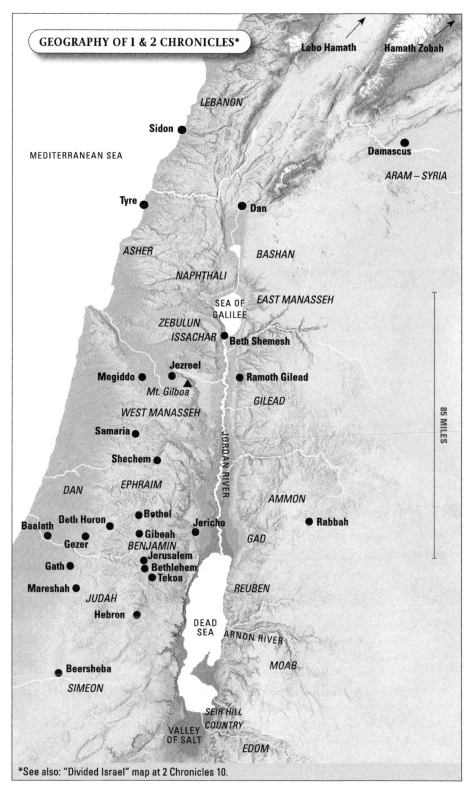

GEOGRAPHY OF 1 & 2 CHRONICLES*

Lebo Hamath

Hamath Zobah

LEBANON

Sidon

MEDITERRANEAN SEA

Damascus

ARAM – SYRIA

Tyre

Dan

ASHER

BASHAN

NAPHTHALI

EAST MANASSEH

SEA OF GALILEE

ZEBULUN

ISSACHAR

Beth Shemesh

Jezreel

Megiddo

Ramoth Gilead

Mt. Gilboa

GILEAD

WEST MANASSEH

Samaria

85 MILES

Shechem

JORDAN RIVER

DAN

EPHRAIM

AMMON

Bethel

Jericho

Baalath

Beth Horon

Rabbah

Gibeah

GAD

Gezer

BENJAMIN

Gath

Jerusalem

Bethlehem

Mareshah

Tekoa

REUBEN

JUDAH

Hebron

DEAD SEA

ARNON RIVER

Beersheba

MOAB

SIMEON

SEIR HILL COUNTRY

VALLEY OF SALT

EDOM

*See also: "Divided Israel" map at 2 Chronicles 10.

Note on Genealogies

The genealogical relationships in chapters 1–9 are not always certain because the text sometimes presents names without mentioning relationship. It is often unclear whether a person is the son or sibling of the person preceding their name in the text. For instance, the persons listed in 1 Chronicles 7:24–27 are named as children of Ephraim in some translations and as a list of several generations (each the father of the next) in others. Some genealogies appear to be fragments, unrelated to any other.

Key to Genealogical Tables

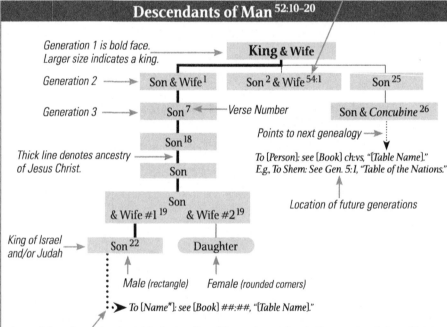

Verse References: If a box or line of text does not have a verse reference, the information comes from the last verse referenced to its left or above it.

Sexual Partners: Wives are in roman typeface, other sexual partners in italics. If a man has children by more than one partner, the partners are in bold typeface.

Dual Relationship: A double arrow (◄—►) connecting two boxes with the same name indicates two relationships (e.g., daughter of one person, wife of another).

Persons Not Listed: Ancient genealogies commonly omit persons and/or generations.

Multiple Genealogies on the same page are separated by double lines.

* Name of the last ancestor of Christ in the referenced table.

1 Chronicles

Part 1. Genealogies

From Adam to Abraham [1:1–27; 4:5–8]

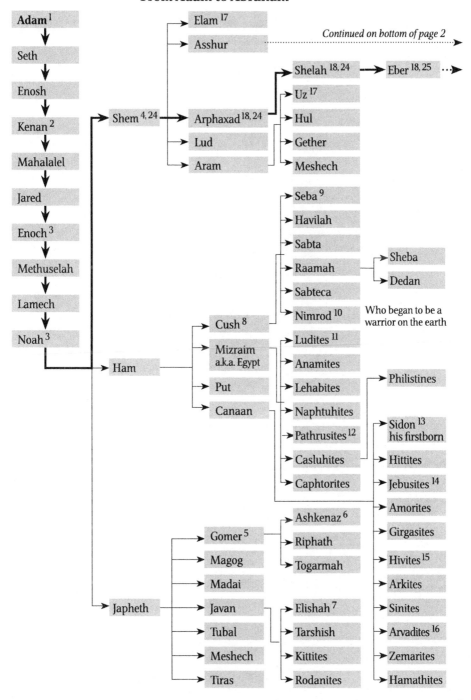

Continued on bottom of page 2

Nimrod [10] — Who began to be a warrior on the earth

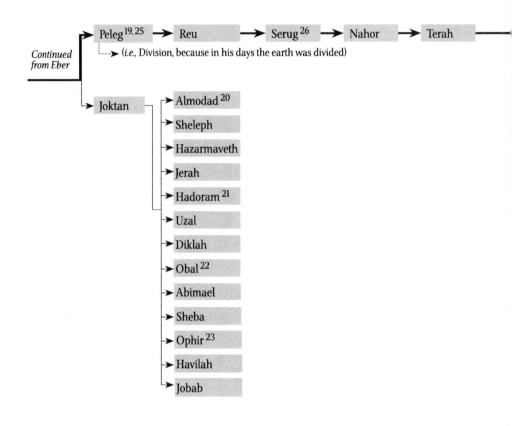

Continued from Eber

Peleg [19, 25] → Reu → Serug [26] → Nahor → Terah →

⤏ (*i.e.*, Division, because in his days the earth was divided)

Joktan →
- Almodad [20]
- Sheleph
- Hazarmaveth
- Jerah
- Hadoram [21]
- Uzal
- Diklah
- Obal [22]
- Abimael
- Sheba
- Ophir [23]
- Havilah
- Jobab

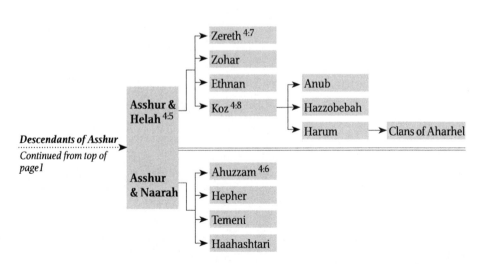

Descendants of Asshur

Continued from top of page 1

Asshur & Helah [4:5] →
- Zereth [4:7]
- Zohar
- Ethnan
- Koz [4:8] →
  - Anub
  - Hazzobebah
  - Harum → Clans of Aharhel

Asshur & Naarah →
- Ahuzzam [4:6]
- Hepher
- Temeni
- Haahashtari

Descendants of Abraham [1:27–37]

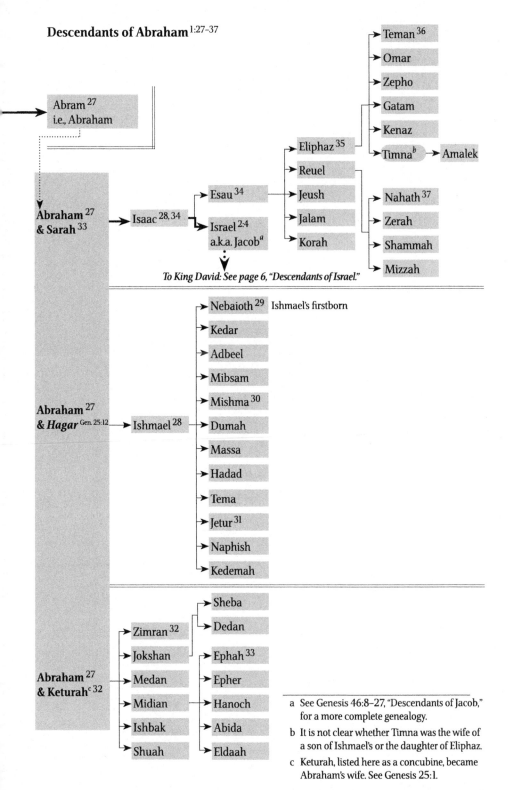

Abram [27]
i.e., Abraham

Abraham [27] & Sarah [33]

Isaac [28, 34]

Esau [34]

Israel [2:4] a.k.a. Jacob[a]

To King David: See page 6, "Descendants of Israel."

Eliphaz [35]
Reuel
Jeush
Jalam
Korah

Teman [36]
Omar
Zepho
Gatam
Kenaz
Timna[b] → Amalek

Nahath [37]
Zerah
Shammah
Mizzah

Abraham [27] & *Hagar* Gen. 25:12

Ishmael [28]

Nebaioth [29]   Ishmael's firstborn
Kedar
Adbeel
Mibsam
Mishma [30]
Dumah
Massa
Hadad
Tema
Jetur [31]
Naphish
Kedemah

Abraham [27] & Keturah[c] [32]

Zimran [32]
Jokshan
Medan
Midian
Ishbak
Shuah

Sheba
Dedan
Ephah [33]
Epher
Hanoch
Abida
Eldaah

a See Genesis 46:8–27, "Descendants of Jacob," for a more complete genealogy.

b It is not clear whether Timna was the wife of a son of Ishmael's or the daughter of Eliphaz.

c Keturah, listed here as a concubine, became Abraham's wife. See Genesis 25:1.

3

Descendants of Seir[a] 1:38–42

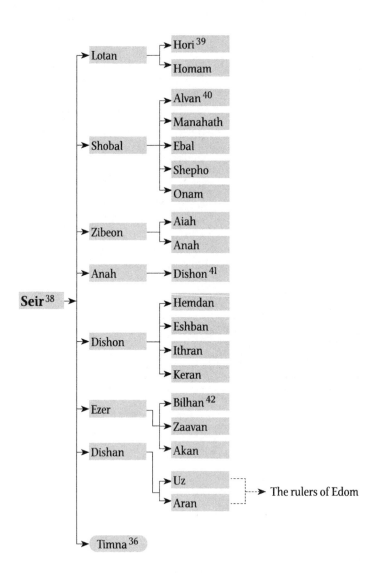

a   See also, Genesis 36:20–30.

[43] These are the kings who reigned in Edom before a king reigned over the Israelites. [44-50] Each king died, and the next king[a] ruled in his place.

King	Son of	His City or Land	*Other Information*
Bela	Beor	Dinhabah	
Jobab [44]	Zerah	Bozrah	
Husham [45]		Land of Teman	
Hadad [46]	Bedad	Avith*	Bedad defeated Midian in the territory of Moab. Hadad became king in his place.
Samlah [47]		Masrekah*	
Shaul [48]		Rehoboth on the river*	
Baal-Hanan [49]	Acbor		
Hadad [50]		Pau[b]*	His wife's name was Mehetabel daughter of Matred, daughter of Me-Zahab.

The location of these cities is unknown.

[51] Then Hadad died.

These were the chiefs of Edom:

Timna	Pinon
Alvah	Kenaz [53]
Jetheth	Teman
Oholibamah [52]	Mibzar
Elah	Magdiel [54]
	Iram

---

a   "The next king": In the Hebrew text, the name of the next king (not the phrase "the next king") is provided in verses 44–50.

b   From many ancient manuscripts; Masoretic text: "Pai."

Descendants of Israel[a 2:1–41]

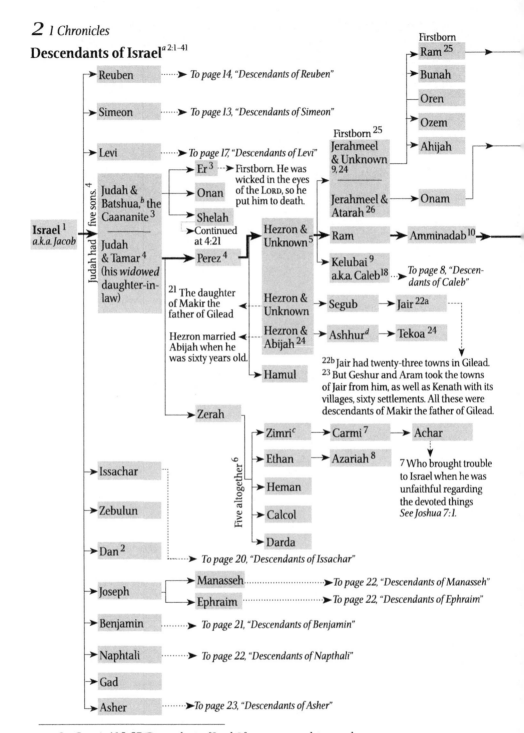

Firstborn
Ram[25]
Bunah
Oren
Ozem
Ahijah

Israel[1]
a.k.a. Jacob

Judah had {five sons.[4]}

Reuben ········► *To page 14, "Descendants of Reuben"*

Simeon ········► *To page 13, "Descendants of Simeon"*

Levi ········► *To page 17, "Descendants of Levi"*

Judah & Batshua,[b] the Caananite[3]

Judah & Tamar[4] (his *widowed* daughter-in-law)

Er[3] ····► Firstborn. He was wicked in the eyes of the LORD, so he put him to death.

Onan

Shelah
►Continued at 4:21

Perez[4]

Firstborn[25]
Jerahmeel & Unknown[9, 24]

Jerahmeel & Atarah[26] ──► Onam

Hezron & Unknown[5] ──► Ram ──► Amminadab[10] ►

Kelubai[9] a.k.a. Caleb[18] ····► *To page 8, "Descendants of Caleb"*

21 The daughter of Makir the father of Gilead ◄········

Hezron & Unknown ──► Segub ──► Jair[22a]

Hezron married Abijah when he was sixty years old. ◄········

Hezron & Abijah[24] ──► Ashhur[d] ──► Tekoa[24]

Hamul

22b Jair had twenty-three towns in Gilead. 23 But Geshur and Aram took the towns of Jair from him, as well as Kenath with its villages, sixty settlements. All these were descendants of Makir the father of Gilead.

Zerah

{Five altogether[6]}

Zimri[c] ──► Carmi[7] ──► Achar

Ethan ──► Azariah[8]

Heman

Calcol

Darda

7 Who brought trouble to Israel when he was unfaithful regarding the devoted things *See Joshua 7:1.*

Issachar

Zebulun

Dan[2] ········► *To page 20, "Descendants of Issachar"*

Joseph
Manasseh ···········►*To page 22, "Descendants of Manasseh"*
Ephraim ···········►*To page 22, "Descendants of Ephraim"*

Benjamin ········► *To page 21, "Descendants of Benjamin"*

Naphtali ········► *To page 22, "Descendants of Napthali"*

Gad

Asher ········►*To page 23, "Descendants of Asher"*

---

a   See Genesis 46:8–27, "Descendants of Jacob," for a more complete genealogy.

b   Or "and the daughter of Shua."

c   Called Zabdi in Joshua 7:1.

d   The Hebrew is uncertain. It may be, as depicted here, that Ashhur was Hezron's son born after Hezron died in Caleb Ephrathah. Or it may be as annotated at 1 Chronicles 2:24 in "Descendants of Caleb" on page 9.

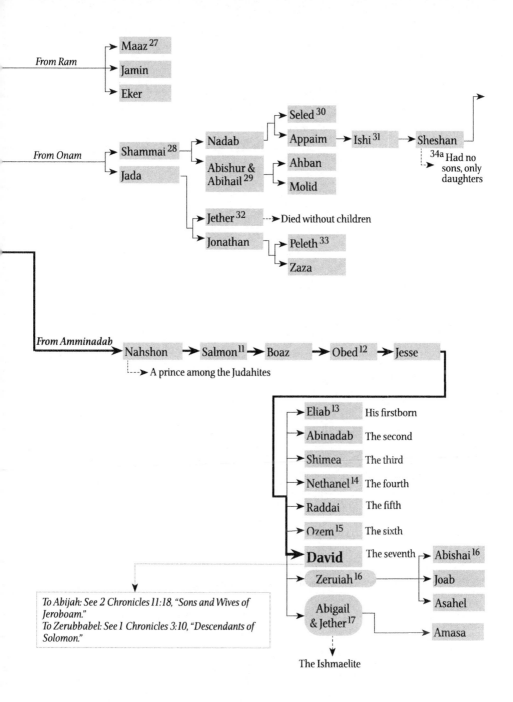

From Ram → Maaz [27]
→ Jamin
→ Eker

From Onam → Shammai [28] → Nadab → Seled [30]
→ Appaim → Ishi [31] → Sheshan
[34a] Had no sons, only daughters

Abishur & Abihail [29] → Ahban
→ Molid

Jada

Jether [32] ---→ Died without children

Jonathan → Peleth [33]
→ Zaza

From Amminadab → Nahshon → Salmon [11] → Boaz → Obed [12] → Jesse
----→ A prince among the Judahites

Eliab [13]   His firstborn
Abinadab   The second
Shimea   The third
Nethanel [14] The fourth
Raddai   The fifth
Ozem [15]   The sixth
David   The seventh → Abishai [16]
Zeruiah [16] → Joab
→ Asahel
Abigail & Jether [17] → Amasa

To Abijah: See 2 Chronicles 11:18, "Sons and Wives of Jeroboam."
To Zerubbabel: See 1 Chronicles 3:10, "Descendants of Solomon."

The Ishmaelite

7

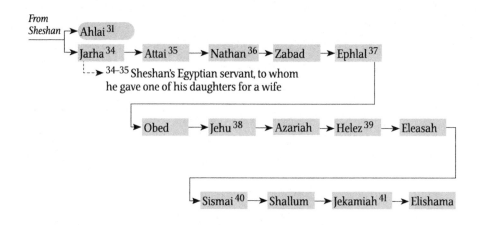

From Sheshan

Ahlai [31]

Jarha [34] → Attai [35] → Nathan [36] → Zabad → Ephlal [37]

[34-35] Sheshan's Egyptian servant, to whom he gave one of his daughters for a wife

Obed → Jehu [38] → Azariah → Helez [39] → Eleasah

Sismai [40] → Shallum → Jekamiah [41] → Elishama

Descendants of Caleb [2:18-20, 24, 42-55; 4:4]
Continued from "Caleb" at 2:18 on page 6

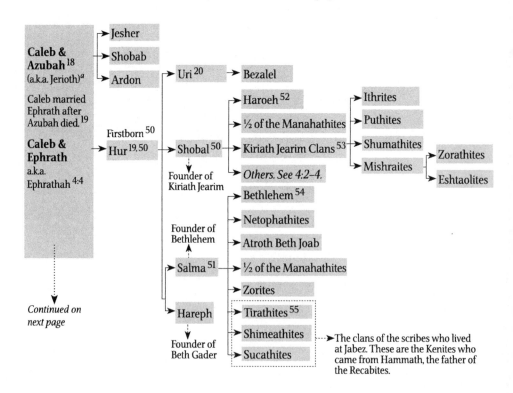

Caleb & Azubah [18]
(a.k.a. Jerioth)[a]

Caleb married Ephrath after Azubah died. [19]

Caleb & Ephrath
a.k.a. Ephrathah [4:4]

Continued on next page

Jesher

Shobab

Ardon → Uri [20] → Bezalel

Firstborn [50]

Hur [19, 50] → Shobal [50] → Haroeh [52] → Ithrites

½ of the Manahathites → Puthites

Kiriath Jearim Clans [53] → Shumathites → Zorathites

Mishraites → Eshtaolites

Others. See 4:2-4.

Founder of Kiriath Jearim

Founder of Bethlehem

Salma [51] → Bethlehem [54]

Netophathites

Atroth Beth Joab

½ of the Manahathites

Zorites

Hareph → Tirathites [55]

Shimeathites

Founder of Beth Gader

Sucathites

The clans of the scribes who lived at Jabez. These are the Kenites who came from Hammath, the father of the Recabites.

---

a   The text is unclear. Jerioth may be an alternate name for Azubah or a daughter, a concubine, or another wife of Caleb.

Descendants of Caleb *continued*

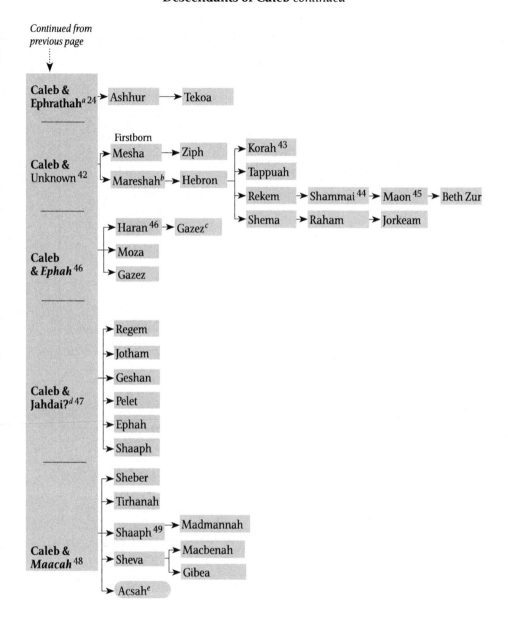

Continued from previous page

Caleb & Ephrathah[a] 24 → Ashhur → Tekoa

Caleb & Unknown 42

Firstborn
→ Mesha → Ziph
→ Mareshah[b] → Hebron

→ Korah 43
→ Tappuah
→ Rekem → Shammai 44 → Maon 45 → Beth Zur
→ Shema → Raham → Jorkeam

Caleb & *Ephah* 46
→ Haran 46 → Gazez[c]
→ Moza
→ Gazez

Caleb & Jahdai?[d] 47
→ Regem
→ Jotham
→ Geshan
→ Pelet
→ Ephah
→ Shaaph

Caleb & *Maacah* 48
→ Sheber
→ Tirhanah
→ Shaaph 49 → Madmannah
→ Sheva → Macbenah
→ Gibea
→ Acsah[e]

---

a   The Hebrew is unclear. It may be that, as depicted here, Ashhur was Caleb's son, born after he slept with (and possibly married) Ephrathah (a.k.a. Ephrath) after his father Hezron died. Or it may be as annotated at 1 Chronicles 2:24 in "Descendants of Israel" in footnote d on page 6.

b   The Hebrew is unclear. Mareshah may be the son of Ziph.

c   The Hebrew is unclear. Either Haran fathered this Gazez or adopted his younger brother.

d   Jahdai's position is unclear (possibly a wife or concubine or a son of Caleb who fathered six sons).

e   The Hebrew is unclear regarding Acsah's mother.

Descendants of David [3:1-9]

[1, 4a] Six were born to him at Hebron, where he reigned for seven years and six months. [9] All these were the sons of David, besides the sons by his concubines, and Tamar was their sister.

Birth Order	Son	Mother
1	Amnon [1]	Ahinoam the Jezreelite
2	Daniel	Abigail the Carmelite
3	Absalom [2]	Maacah daughter of Talmai, king of Geshur
4	Adonijah	Haggith
5	Shephatiah [3]	Abital
6	Ithream	Eglah, David's wife

[5a] *These* were born to him in Jerusalem, [4b] where he reigned for thirty-three years.

Birth Order	Son	Mother
1	Shimea[a] [5b]	Bathsheba[b] daughter of Ammiel
2	Shobab	
3	Nathan	
4	**Solomon** ———	

[8b] Nine *other sons*

1	Ibhar [6]	*Unknown*
2	Elishua	*Unknown*
3	Eliphelet	*Unknown*
4	Nogah [7]	*Unknown*
5	Nepheg	*Unknown*
6	Japhia	*Unknown*
7	Elishama [8a]	*Unknown*
8	Eliada	*Unknown*
9	Eliphelet	*Unknown*

a Referred to as "Shammua" in 2 Samuel 5:14.
b Literally, "Bathshua," an alternate spelling of Bathsheba.

Descendants of Solomon [3:10–24]

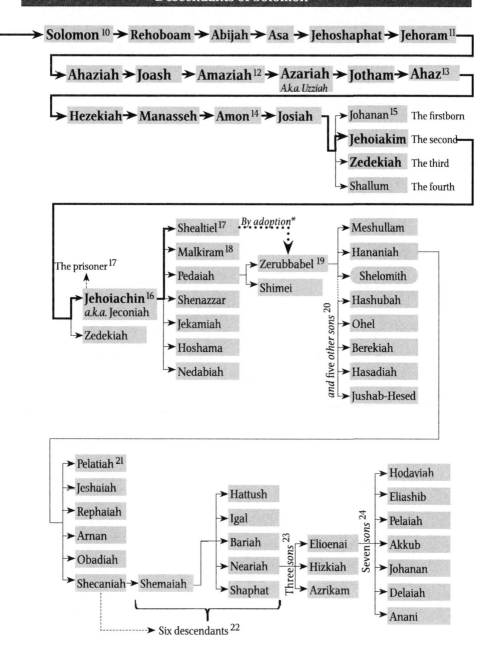

* "By adoption": an assumption based upon these references to Shealtiel as Zerubbabel's father: Ezra 3:2; 5:2; Nehemiah 1:1; and Haggai 1:1.

Descendants of Judah

[1] *Some of* the descendants of Judah were Perez, Hezron, Carmi, Hur, and Shobal. *Others include:*

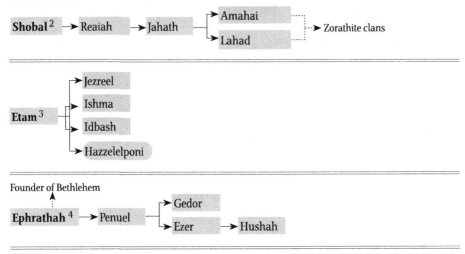

4:5–8 are at "Descendants of Asshur" on page 2

[9] Jabez was more honorable than his brothers. His mother named him Jabez, saying, "Because I gave birth *to him* in pain." [10] Jabez called on the God of Israel, saying, "Oh that you would bless me indeed and enlarge my territory, and that your hand would be with me! Keep me from disaster, so I may not have pain." And God granted what he had requested.

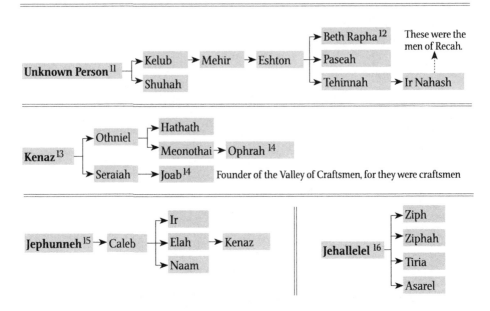

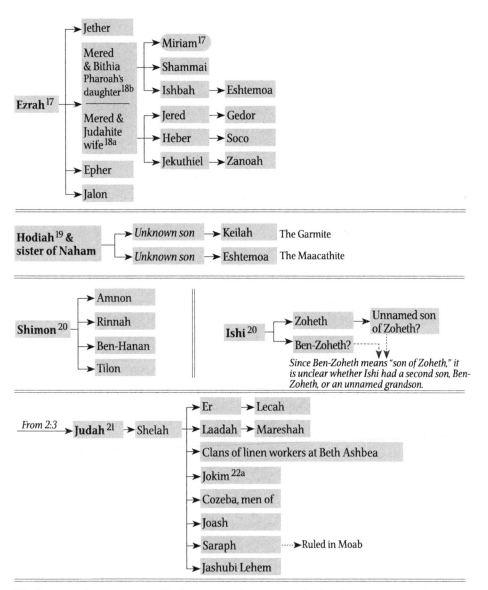

Ezrah [17]
- Jether
- Mered & Bithia Pharoah's daughter [18b]
  - Miriam [17]
  - Shammai
  - Ishbah → Eshtemoa
- Mered & Judahite wife [18a]
  - Jered → Gedor
  - Heber → Soco
  - Jekuthiel → Zanoah
- Epher
- Jalon

Hodiah [19] & sister of Naham
- Unknown son → Keilah — The Garmite
- Unknown son → Eshtemoa — The Maacathite

Shimon [20]
- Amnon
- Rinnah
- Ben-Hanan
- Tilon

Ishi [20]
- Zoheth → Unnamed son of Zoheth?
- Ben-Zoheth?

Since Ben-Zoheth means "son of Zoheth," it is unclear whether Ishi had a second son, Ben-Zoheth, or an unnamed grandson.

From 2:3 → Judah [21] → Shelah
- Er → Lecah
- Laadah → Mareshah
- Clans of linen workers at Beth Ashbea
- Jokim [22a]
- Cozeba, men of
- Joash
- Saraph ┈┈→ Ruled in Moab
- Jashubi Lehem

[22b] The records are ancient. [23] They[a] were the potters who lived in Netaim and Gederah. They stayed there to work for the king.

Descendants of Simeon

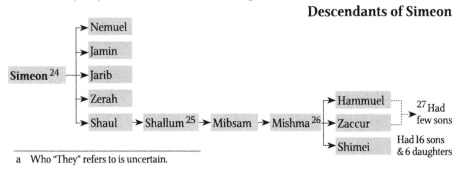

Simeon [24]
- Nemuel
- Jamin
- Jarib
- Zerah
- Shaul → Shallum [25] → Mibsam → Mishma [26]
  - Hammuel ┈┈┐
  - Zaccur ┈┈┴→ [27] Had few sons
  - Shimei — Had 16 sons & 6 daughters

---

a   Who "They" refers to is uncertain.

^{27} Shimei had sixteen sons and six daughters, but his brothers did not have many sons, so all their clans did not become as numerous as the Judahites. ^{28} They lived in Beersheba, Moladah, Hazar Shual, ^{29} Bilhah, Ezem, Tolad, ^{30} Bethuel, Hormah, Ziklag, ^{31} Beth Marcaboth, Hazar Susim, Beth Biri, and Shaaraim. These were their towns until David became king. ^{32} Their villages were Etam, Ain, Rimmon, Token, and Ashan: five towns ^{33} and all the settlements that surrounded these towns as far as Baalath. These were their dwelling places, and they kept a genealogical record. ^{38a} These were recorded^a as leaders of their clans:

Meshobab ^{34}	Jaakobah
Jamlech	Jeshohaiah
Joshah son of Amaziah	Asaiah
Joel ^{35}	Adiel
Jehu son of Joshibiah, son of Seraiah, son of Asiel	Jesimiel
	Benaiah
Elioenai ^{36}	Ziza son of Shiphi, son of Allon, son of Jedaiah, son of Shimri, son of Shemaiah ^{37}

^{38b} Their families increased greatly. ^{39} They went to the outskirts^b of Gerar,^{c} in the east *end* of the valley to seek pasture for their flocks. ^{40} They found lush, nutritious pasture with spacious, quiet, tranquil land. Some Hamites had lived there formerly. ^{41} These, who had been registered by name, went there in the days of Hezekiah king of Judah and defeated the Hamites in their tents and the Meunites who were found there. They completely destroyed them, as it is today. They settled in their place, for there was pasture for their flocks.

^{42} Some of the Simeonites, five hundred troops, went to the Seir hill country, with Pelatiah, Neariah, Rephaiah, Uzziel—the sons of Ishi—leading them. ^{43} They defeated the last of the surviving Amalekites and settled there, as it is today.

5 *1 Chronicles*

Descendants of Reuben

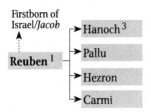

^{1} Reuben was the firstborn of Israel. *However, because* he defiled his father's *marriage* bed, his birthright^d was given to the sons of Joseph son of Israel. Therefore he is not listed according to his birthright. ^{2} Though Judah was stronger than his brothers and leaders came from him, the rights of the firstborn went to Joseph.

---

a Literally, "The coming in by names."
b Literally, "the entrance."
c From the Septuagint; Masoretic text: Gedor.
d "Birthright": the privileges given to one by birth; in this case, the rights of the firstborn.

Joel [4]
- Shemaiah
- Gog
- Shemei [4] (a.k.a. Shema [8]) → Azaz → Bela
- Micah [5]
- Reaiah
- Baal
- Beerah [6]

Beerah, a leader of the Reubenites, was taken into exile by Tiglath-Pileser king of Assyria.[a] [7] His kinsmen, listed by families in their genealogical records, were

> Jeiel the chief,
> Zechariah,

[8] Bela son of Azaz, son of Shema, son of Joel,

> who lived in Aroer up to Nebo and Baal Meon, [9] living to the east
> up to the edge of the desert *that goes* to the Euphrates River,
> for their livestock had increased in the land of Gilead.

[10] In Saul's time they waged war with the Hagrites, who fell by their hands. Then they occupied the homes of the Hagrites in all the land east of Gilead.

Settlements of Reuben, Gad, and Manasseh [5:10b–17, 23–24a]			
Tribe/Clan	**Location**	**Chiefs**	**Kinsmen** by families
Reubenites [1]	*Gilead &* East of Gilead [10b]	Jeiel [7]	
Gadites [11]	[11] Opposite the Reubenites, in the land of Bashan up to Salekah. [16] They lived in Gilead, in Bashan and its villages, in all the pasturelands around Sharon as far as their borders.	[12] Joel (1st) Shapham (2nd) Then Janai and Shaphat in Bashan.	[13] Michael, Meshullam, Sheba, Jorai, Jacan, Zia, and Eber, seven total, [14] *all* descendants of Abihail son of Huri, son of Jaroah, son of Gilead, son of Michael, son of Jeshishai, son of Jahdo, son of Buz. [15] Ahi son of Abdiel, son of Guni, was the head of their family. [17] All of them were registered in the days of Jotham king of Judah and Jeroboam *II* king of *Northern* Israel.
Manasseh, half-tribe [23]	From Bashan to Baal Hermon and Senir (Mount Hermon), for they were many.	[24a] Epher, Ishi, Eliel, Azriel, Jeremiah, Hodaviah, Jahdiel	

---

a   See 1 Chronicles 5:26.

Wars of Reuben, Gad, and Manasseh Before Taken into Exile

[18] The Reubenites, Gadites, and the half-tribe of Manasseh together had 44,760 men trained for battle who could go to war, who wielded shields and swords, and who could draw the bow. [19] They waged war with the Hagrites, Jetur, Naphish, and Nodab. [20] Since they cried out to God during the battle, they were helped against them, and the Hagrites and all their allies were given into their hands. He answered their prayers because they relied on him. [21] They captured their *enemies'* livestock: 50,000 camels, 2,000 donkeys, 250,000 sheep, as well as 100,000 people. [22] Many fell slain, for the victory was from God. Then they settled there in *their land* until the exile.

5:23–24a are in the "Settlements" table above

[24b] The chiefs of Manasseh were mighty warriors, men of reputation, and heads of their families. [25] But they were unfaithful to the God of their ancestors and prostituted themselves to the gods of the local peoples, whom God had destroyed right before them. [26] Then the God of Israel moved the spirit of Pul king of Assyria (*also known as* Tiglath-Pileser king of Assyria), who took them all—the Reubenites, the Gadites, and the half-tribe of Manasseh—into exile and brought them to Halah, Habor, Hara, and the Gozan River, *where they are* to this day.

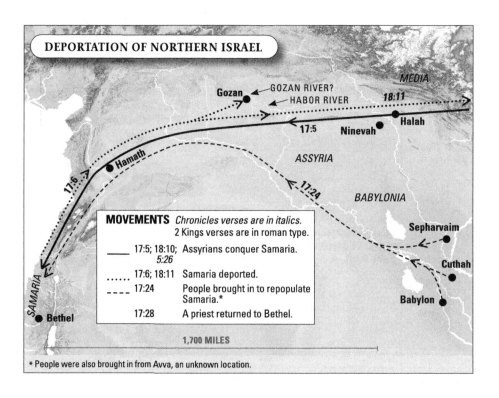

Descendants of Levi

[19b] These are the clans of Levi according to their ancestries.
[48] Their relatives, the other Levites, were given all the other duties of the tabernacle, the temple of God. [49] Aaron and his descendants presented offerings on the altar of burnt offering and on the altar of incense for all the service of the Most Holy Place, and to atone for Israel, according to all the commandments of Moses the servant of God.

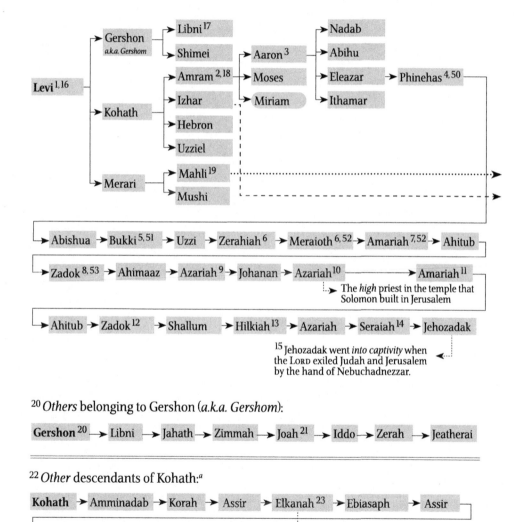

[20] *Others* belonging to Gershon (*a.k.a. Gershom*):

Gershon [20] → Libni → Jahath → Zimmah → Joah [21] → Iddo → Zerah → Jeatherai

[22] *Other* descendants of Kohath:[a]

Kohath → Amminadab → Korah → Assir → Elkanah [23] → Ebiasaph → Assir → Tahath [24] → Uriel → Uzziah → Shaul

To "The descendants of Elkanah."

---

a   The relationships and generations of the people in verses 22–27 are uncertain.

25 The descendants of Elkanah:

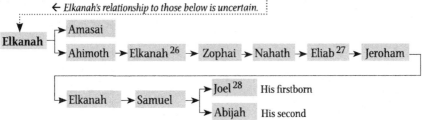

← Elkanah's relationship to those below is uncertain.

Elkanah → Amasai

→ Ahimoth → Elkanah [26] → Zophai → Nahath → Eliab [27] → Jeroham →

→ Elkanah → Samuel → Joel [28] His firstborn

→ Abijah His second

29 *Other* descendants of Merari:

Merari → Mahli → Libni → Shimei → Uzzah → Shimea [30] → Haggiah → Asaiah

Levite Musicians

31 These are the men David put in charge of the service of song in the house of the LORD after the ark rested there. **32** They ministered with song in front of the tabernacle (*i.e.*, the meeting tent) until Solomon built the house of the LORD in Jerusalem. They served according to the regulations.

Kohathites

33a These are the Kohathite men who served along with their sons:

Israel [38] → Levi → **Kohath** → Izhar → Korah [37] → Ebiasaph → Assir → Tahath →
(*a.k.a. Jacob*)

→ Zephaniah [36] → Azariah → Joel → Elkanah → Amasi [35] → Mahath → Elkanah →

→ Zuph → Toah [34] → Eliel → Jeroham → Elkanah → Samuel [33b] → Joel → Heman

The *head* musician ◄┈┄

Gershonites (a.k.a. Gershomites)

Levi [43] → **Gershon** → Jahath → Shimei [42] → Zimmah → Ethan → Adaiah [41] → Zerah →

→ Ethni → Malkijah [40] → Baaseiah → Michael → Shimea [39] → Berekiah → Asaph

His *Gershonite* kinsman stood at his right hand. ◄┈

Merarites

Levi [47] → **Merari** → Mushi → Mahli → Shemer [46] → Bani → Amzi → Hilkiah [45] →

→ Amaziah → Hashabiah → Malluch [44] → Abdi → Kishi → Ethan

His *Merarite* kinsmen were at his left hand. ◄┈

Priests

Aaron [50] → Eleazar → Phinehas → Abishua → Bukki [51] → Uzzi → Zerahiah →

→ Meraioth [52] → Amariah → Ahitub → Zadok [53] → Ahimaaz

[54a] These were their settlements by camp allotted as their territory. [64] The Israelites gave the Levites these cities and their pasturelands.

Receiving Family	Land Given (each with its pasturelands)

Kohath Aaron (from the family of Kohath), for the *first* lot fell to them. [54b, 57a]	In *the territory of* Judah
	  Hebron [55] [56] But Caleb son of Jephunneh was given the town's countryside and its villages.
	  Libnah [57b] Eshtemoa Debir Juttah[a]
	  Jattir Hilen [58] Ashan [59] Beth Shemesh

Some *other* descendants of Kohath [61, 66a, 70b]	From the tribe of Benjamin [60] Gibeon Geba Alemeth[b] Anathoth The cities of all their families numbered thirteen.

	From the territory of the tribe of Ephraim [66b]
	  Shechem, a city of refuge Jokmeam
	    in the hill country [67] Beth Horon [69]
	  Gezer [68] Aijalon
	      Gath Rimmon
	
	Two of the ten cities given by lot from the *territory of* the half-tribe of Manasseh [61]
	  Aner, Bileam [70]

Gershon's descendants [62a, 71a]	Thirteen cities in Bashan were given according to their clans from the tribes of Issachar, Asher, Naphtali, and the half-tribe of Manasseh [62b]
	
	From the half-tribe of Manasseh[c] [71b]
	  Golan in Bashan Ashtaroth
	
	From the tribe of Issachar [72]
	  Kedesh Daberath Ramoth [73] Anem
	
	From the tribe of Asher [74]
	  Mashal Abdon Hukok [75] Rehob
	
	From the tribe of Naphtali [76]
	  Kedesh in Galilee Hammon Kiriathaim

Merari's descendants [63a, 77]	Twelve cities were given according to their clans by lot from the tribes of Reuben, Gad, and Zebulun. [63b] They gave those cities mentioned by name by lot from the tribes of Judah, Simeon, and Benjamin. [65]
	
	From the tribe of Zebulun [77]
	  Jokneam, Kartah,[d] Rimmono, and Tabor
	
	From the tribe of Reuben, east of Jericho and the Jordan River [78]
	  Bezer in the wilderness, Kedemoth, [79] Jahzah, and Mephaath
	
	From the tribe of Gad [80]
	  Ramoth in Gilead, Heshbon, [81] Mahanaim, and Jazer

---

a From the Septuagint.
b From Joshua 21:17.
c Literally, "the family of the half-tribe of Manasseh."
d "Jokneam" and "Kartah" are from the Septuagint.

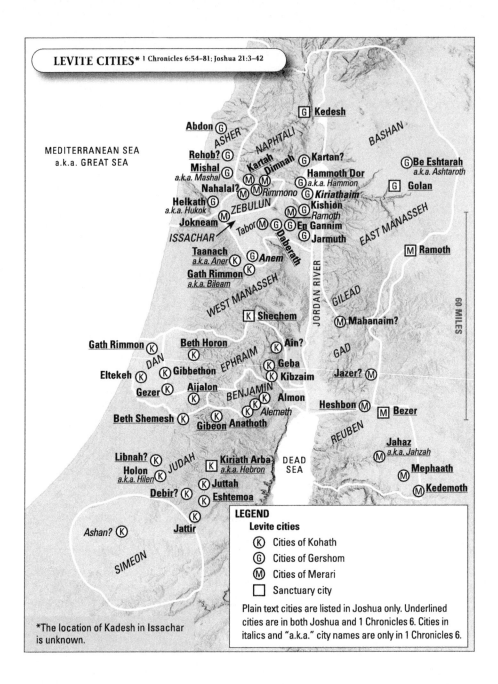

LEVITE CITIES * 1 Chronicles 6:54–81; Joshua 21:3–42

MEDITERRANEAN SEA
a.k.a. GREAT SEA

Ⓖ Kedesh

Abdon Ⓖ

ASHER

NAPHTALI

BASHAN

Rehob? Ⓖ

Kartah

Dimnah Ⓖ Kartan?

Mishal Ⓖ
a.k.a. Mashal

Nahalal? Ⓜ Ⓜ
Rimmono

Ⓜ

Hammoth Dor
Ⓖ *a.k.a. Hammon*

ⒼBeEshtarah
a.k.a. Ashtaroth

Ⓖ Kiriathaim

Ⓖ Golan

Helkath Ⓖ
a.k.a. Hukok

ZEBULUN

Ⓜ Kishion

Ⓜ Ⓖ
Ramoth

Jokneam

Tabor Ⓜ ⒼⒼ En Gannim

EAST MANASSEH

ISSACHAR

Ⓖ Jarmuth

Taanach
a.k.a. Aner Ⓚ Ⓖ *Anem*

Daberath

Ⓜ Ramoth

Gath Rimmon Ⓚ
a.k.a. Bileam

WEST MANASSEH

JORDAN RIVER

GILEAD

Ⓚ Shechem

Ⓜ Mahanaim?

Gath Rimmon Ⓚ

Beth Horon
Ⓚ

Ⓚ Ain?

GAD

Eltekeh Ⓚ

DAN

Ⓚ Gibbethon

EPHRAIM

Ⓚ Geba

Jazer? Ⓜ

Gezer Ⓚ

Aijalon

Ⓚ Kibzaim

BENJAMIN

Beth Shemesh Ⓚ

ⓀⓀ Almon
ⓀⓀ *Alemeth*

Heshbon Ⓜ

Ⓜ Bezer

Gibeon Anathoth

REUBEN

Jahaz
Ⓜ *a.k.a. Jahzah*

Libnah? Ⓚ

JUDAH

Kiriath Arba
Ⓚ *a.k.a. Hebron*

DEAD
SEA

Ⓜ Mephaath

Holon Ⓚ
a.k.a. Hilen

Ⓚ Juttah

Ⓜ Kedemoth

Debir? Ⓚ

Ⓚ Eshtemoa

Ashan? Ⓚ

Ⓚ
Jattir

LEGEND

Levite cities

Ⓚ Cities of Kohath

Ⓖ Cities of Gershom

Ⓜ Cities of Merari

☐ Sanctuary city

SIMEON

Plain text cities are listed in Joshua only. Underlined cities are in both Joshua and 1 Chronicles 6. Cities in italics and "a.k.a." city names are only in 1 Chronicles 6.

60 MILES

*The location of Kadesh in Issachar is unknown.

Descendants of Issachar

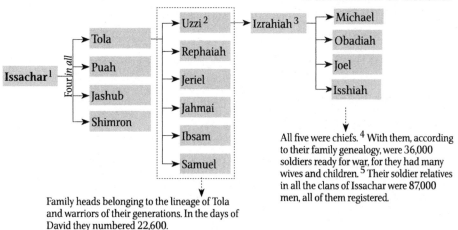

All five were chiefs. **4** With them, according to their family genealogy, were 36,000 soldiers ready for war, for they had many wives and children. **5** Their soldier relatives in all the clans of Issachar were 87,000 men, all of them registered.

Family heads belonging to the lineage of Tola and warriors of their generations. In the days of David they numbered 22,600.

Descendants of Benjamin

Five family heads who were warriors. They had 22,034 warriors listed in their genealogy.

9 *Nine* family heads listed in their genealogy according to generations. They had 20,200 warriors.

11 All these were the descendants of Jediael and family heads. There were 17,200 warriors who went out to battle with them.

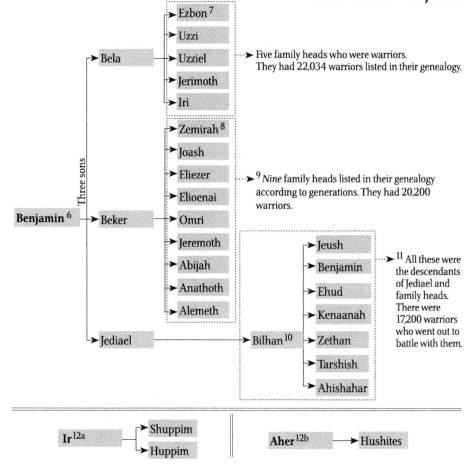

Descendants of Naphtali

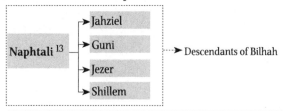

Descendants of Manasseh

^{15a} Makir took a wife from among the Huppites and Shuppites.

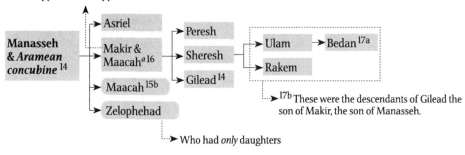

Descendants of Ephraim

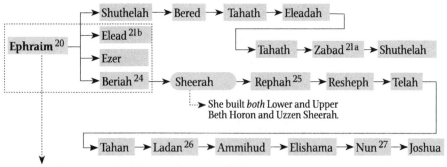

^{21b} *Ephraim's sons* Ezer and Elead were killed by the native-born men of Gath when they went down to steal their livestock. ²² Their father Ephraim mourned for many days, and his relatives came to console him. ²³ Then he made love to^b his wife, and she conceived and bore a son. He named him Beriah, (*i.e.*, Tragedy), for disaster had

---

a   Makir had both a sister and a wife named Maacah.
b   Literally, "went in to."

come to his family. [28] Ephraim's property and dwellings were Bethel and its villages, Naaran to the east, Gezer and its villages to the west, and Shechem and its villages up to Ayyah and its villages. [29] Along the border with the Manassites were Beth Shan and its villages, Taanach and its villages, Megiddo and its villages, and Dor and its villages. The descendants of Joseph son of Israel (*a.k.a. Jacob*) lived in these towns.

Descendants of Asher

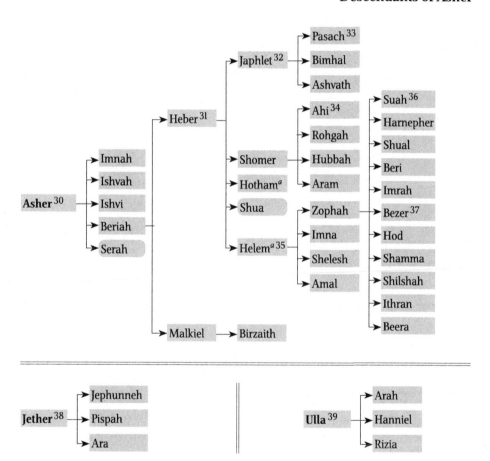

[40] All these were the descendants of Asher, family heads, choice warriors, leaders among the chiefs. They were registered in the army for war, numbering 26,000 men.

---

a   Some scholars believe Hotham and Helem may be the same person.

Descendants of Benjamin

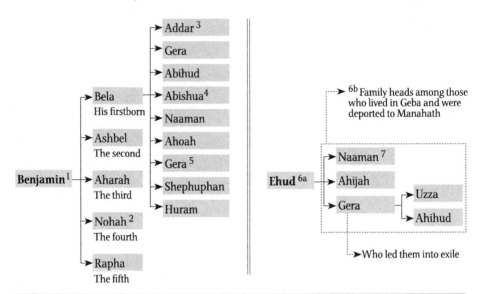

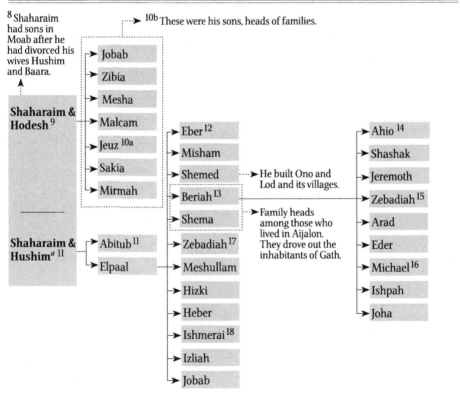

---

a   Whether this is the Hushim he divorced (see verse 8) or another is unknown.

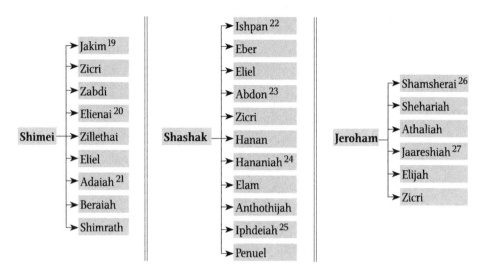

Shimei → Jakim [19], Zicri, Zabdi, Elienai [20], Zillethai, Eliel, Adaiah [21], Beraiah, Shimrath

Shashak → Ishpan [22], Eber, Eliel, Abdon [23], Zicri, Hanan, Hananiah [24], Elam, Anthothijah, Iphdeiah [25], Penuel

Jeroham → Shamsherai [26], Shehariah, Athaliah, Jaareshiah [27], Elijah, Zicri

[28] These were all family heads in their generations and chiefs. They lived in Jerusalem.

Descendants of Saul
Verse numbers in italics are from chapter 9

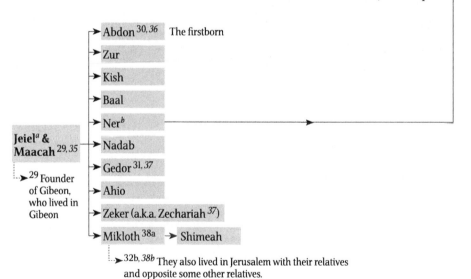

Jeiel[a] & Maacah [29, 35]

[29] Founder of Gibeon, who lived in Gibeon

→ Abdon [30, 36] The firstborn
→ Zur
→ Kish
→ Baal
→ Ner[b]
→ Nadab
→ Gedor [31, 37]
→ Ahio
→ Zeker (a.k.a. Zechariah [37])
→ Mikloth [38a] → Shimeah

[32b, 38b] They also lived in Jerusalem with their relatives and opposite some other relatives.

---

a From the Septuagint.
b From the Septuagint.

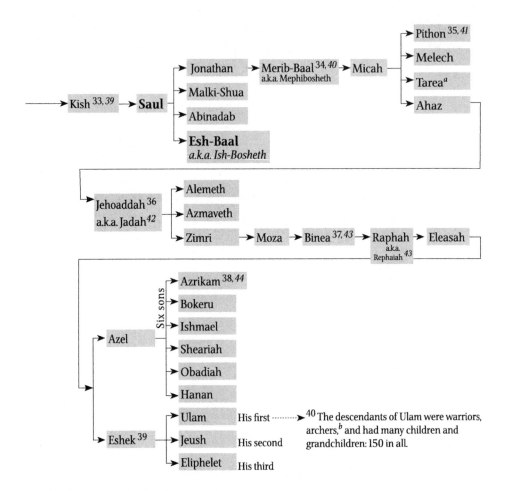

Kish [33, 39] → **Saul**
- Jonathan → Merib-Baal [34, 40] a.k.a. Mephibosheth → Micah
  - Pithon [35, 41]
  - Melech
  - Tarea[a]
  - Ahaz
- Malki-Shua
- Abinadab
- **Esh-Baal** a.k.a. Ish-Bosheth

Jehoaddah [36] a.k.a. Jadah[42]
- Alemeth
- Azmaveth
- Zimri → Moza → Binea [37, 43] → Raphah a.k.a. Rephaiah [43] → Eleasah

Azel — Six sons
- Azrikam [38, 44]
- Bokeru
- Ishmael
- Sheariah
- Obadiah
- Hanan

Eshek [39]
- Ulam — His first ········→ [40] The descendants of Ulam were warriors, archers,[b] and had many children and grandchildren: 150 in all.
- Jeush — His second
- Eliphelet — His third

All these were Benjamites.

---

a   "Tahrea" in 1 Chronicles 9:41.
b   Literally, "who drew the bow."

[1] All Israel registered themselves. Look, they are written down in the book Kings of Israel. Judah was exiled to Babylon because the people were unfaithful. [2] The first ones to resettle their property in their cities were some Israelites—priests, Levites, and temple servants.

Leaders Who Resettled Jerusalem [9:3-34]	

[3] Some descendants of Judah, Benjamin, Ephraim, and Manasseh resettled in Jerusalem.

Group	Family Heads and Members
Judahites	690 *kinsmen* [6b]
	Uthai son of Ammihud, son of Omri, son of Imri, son of Bani, son of Perez, son of Judah [4]
Shilonites [5]	Asaiah the firstborn and his sons
Zerahites [6a]	Jeuel
Benjamites [7]	956 kinsmen [9]
	Sallu son of Meshullam, son of Hodaviah, son of Hassenuah [7]
	Ibneiah son of Jeroham [8]
	Elah son of Uzzi, son of Micri
	Meshullam son of Shephatiah, son of Reuel, son of Ibnijah
Priests [10a]	1,760 men [13a]
	Jedaiah [10b]
	Jehoiarib
	Jakin
	Adaiah son of Jeroham, son of Pashhur, son of Malkijah [12]
	Maasai son of Adiel, son of Jahzerah, son of Meshullam, son of Meshillemith, son of Immer
	Also their relatives, the heads of families, capable men for the responsibility of the service in the temple of God [13b]
Leader of the temple of God [11]	Azariah son of Hilkiah, son of Meshullam, son of Zadok, son of Meraioth, son of Ahitub
Levites [14]	These were the family heads of the Levites according to their generations, chiefs who lived in Jerusalem. [34]
	Shemaiah son of Hasshub, son of Azrikam, son of Hashabiah, from the descendants of Merari [14]
	Bakbakkar [15]
	Heresh
	Galal
	Mattaniah son of Mica, son of Zicri, son of Asaph
	Obadiah son of Shemaiah, son of Galal, son of Jeduthun [16]
	Berekiah son of Asa, son of Elkanah, who lived in the villages of the Netophathites

Levites who were **Gatekeepers**[17] for the camp of the sons of Levi[18b]	212 in all[22]
	They were registered by their genealogy in their villages. David and Samuel the prophet appointed them to positions of trust.
	Shallum, head gatekeeper[17]
	Akkub
	Talmon
	Ahiman and their relatives
	Up to now they were stationed at the King's Gate to the east.[18a]
	[23] Gatekeepers and their descendants guarded the gates of the temple, the house of the tent. [24] They were on all four sides: east, west, north, and south. [25] Their relatives in their villages took seven-day turns[a] with them. [26] The four chief gatekeepers, who were Levites, were entrusted with the rooms and treasuries in the temple. [27] They spent the night surrounding the temple, for they were responsible to watch over it and open it each morning.
Levites who were **Guards** of the meeting tent entrance[19b, 21b]	Shallum son of Kore, son of Ebiasaph, son of Korah[19]
	Shallum's relatives in his father's family, the Korahites, *served* as their ancestors had.
	Previously Phinehas son of Eleazar had been their leader, and the LORD was with him.[20]
	Zechariah son of Meshelemiah, at the tent of meeting entrance[21a]

[28] Some of the guards were in charge of the utensils used for worship. They counted them when they were brought out and when they were returned. [29] Others were appointed over the furniture and the *other* articles in the sanctuary, as well as the fine flour, wine, olive oil, incense, and spices. [30] Some of the priests mixed the spices.

[31] Mattithiah, one of the Levites, who was the firstborn of Shallum the Korahite, was responsible for baking things in pans. [32] Some of their relatives, the Kohathites, were in charge of preparing the showbread for every Sabbath.

[33] The singers, family heads of the Levites, stayed in the rooms *of the temple* and were exempt *from other duties* because they were at work day and night.

9:35–44 are in "Genealogy of Saul" at 8:29

---

a   Literally, "for seven days from time to time."

Part 2. David's Reign

The Death of Saul and His Sons[a]

[1] The Philistines fought against Israel, and the Israelite troops fled before them. They fell slain before them on Mount Gilboa. [2] The Philistines stayed close to Saul and his sons, and they slew Jonathan, Abinadab, and Malki-Shua, the sons of Saul. [3] The battle became so heavy around Saul that *Philistine* archers found him and wounded him. [4] Saul told his armor-bearer, "Draw your sword and stab me with it, so these uncircumcised *brutes don't* come and make sport of me." But the armor-bearer was not willing *to do it* because he was terrified, so Saul took his own sword and fell upon it. [5] When the armor-bearer saw that Saul was dead, he also fell upon his sword and died.

[6] So Saul and his three sons and all his house died together. [7] When all the Israelite *civilians* who were in the valley saw *the army* had retreated and that Saul and his sons were dead, they abandoned their towns and fled. Then the Philistines came and lived in them.

[8] The next day, when the Philistines came to strip the dead, they found Saul and his sons fallen on Mount Gilboa. [9] They stripped him, cut off his head, took his armor, and sent messengers around the land of the Philistines to proclaim the good news to their idols and the people. [10] They put his armor in the temple of their gods and hung his skull in the temple of Dagon.

[11] When all Jabesh Gilead heard all that the Philistines had done to Saul, [12] every warrior got up and took the body of Saul and the bodies of his sons to Jabesh and buried their bones beneath the oak tree at Jabesh. Then they fasted for seven days.

[13] So Saul died because he was unfaithful when he rebelled against the LORD, disregarding the word of the LORD and even consulting the spirits of the dead. [14] He did not seek the LORD, so he put him to death and turned the kingdom over to David son of Jesse.

David Anointed King

[1] All Israel gathered to David at Hebron, saying, "Look, we are your flesh and your blood. [2] In the past, even when Saul was king, you led Israel.[b] The LORD your God said to you, 'You will shepherd my people Israel, and you will be the leader over my people Israel.'" [3] Then all the elders of Israel went to the king at Hebron, and David made a covenant with them before the LORD; and they anointed David king over Israel, according to the word of the LORD through[c] Samuel.

---

a   See also 1 Samuel 31:1–6.
b   Literally, "you were the leader-out and leader-in of Israel."
c   Literally, "by the hand of."

David Captures Jerusalem

[4] David and all Israel went to Jerusalem (that is, Jebus), where the Jebusites inhabited the land. [5] They said to David, "You will not get in here." But David captured the fortress of Zion (that is, the City of David).

[6] David had said, "Whoever strikes the Jebusites first will be the head and commander." And Joab son of Zeruiah went up first, and so he became head *of the army.* [7] David lived in the fortress; therefore, it was renamed the City of David. [8] He built the city all around, from the terraces[a] to the surrounding area. Joab rebuilt[b] the rest of the city. [9] David became greater and greater, and the LORD of Armies was with him.

David's Fighting Men

[10] These are the heads of David's mighty men who, together with all Israel, were with him to make him king and strengthen him in his kingdom, according to the word of the LORD concerning Israel. [11a] This is the roster of David's mighty men:

Leaders of David's Fighting Men [11:11b–47]		
Name	**Position**	**Achievements**
Jashobeam the Hacmonite [11b]	Head *over* the Thirty[c]	Who lifted his spear and killed three hundred at one time
Eleazar son of Dodai the Ahohite [12]	One of the three mighty men	With David at Pas Dammim [13a]
Abishai the brother of Joab [20a]	A chief of the Thirty	*See 11:20–21.*
Benaiah son of Jehoiada [24]		*See 11:22–25.*
Amasai [12:18]	A chief of the Thirty	*See 12:18.*

[13b] At a plot full of barley at Pas Dammin, the people fled before the Philistines; [14] but they made a stand in the middle of the field, defended it, and struck down the Philistines. The LORD saved them with a great victory.

[15] Now three of the thirty chiefs went down to David to the rock at the cave of Adullam, while the Philistines were encamped in the valley of Rephaim. [16] At that time David was in the stronghold, and the Philistines were garrisoned in Bethlehem. [17] David was thirsty and said, "If only someone would bring me water from the cistern in Bethlehem, which is near the gate!" [18] So the three *mighty men* cut their way through the Philistine camp and drew water from the cistern by the gate in Bethlehem. They took it up and brought it to David, but he refused to drink it. He poured it on the ground to the LORD [19] and said, "May the LORD forbid that I should do this before my God. Shall I drink the blood of these men who brought *the water* at the risk of their lives?"[d] So he was not willing to drink it. The three mighty men did these things.

---

a   Literally, "from the *millo.*" The meaning of *millo* is uncertain.
b   Literally, "He revived."
c   "Thirty": from the Syriac; Masoretic text: "Three." Many scholars believe these were the officers.
d   Literally, "of these men against their lives who brought it against their lives?"

²⁰ Abishai the brother of Joab was chief of the Three. He lifted his spear against three hundred and killed them. He had a name among the three *mighty men.* ²¹ He was the most honored of the Three. He was their leader but equal to the Three *in combat.ᵃ*

²² Benaiah son of Jehoiada was a valiant man of many daring deeds from Kabzeel. He struck down two *sons of Ariel* of Moab. He *also* went down into a pit on a snowy day and killed a lion. ²³ He *even* struck down an Egyptian *soldier* who was seven and a half feetᵇ tall. In the Egyptian's hand was a spear with a shaft like a weaver's beam, but Benaiah went down to him with *only* a club. He snatched the spear out of the Egyptian's hand and killed him with his own spear. ²⁴ Benaiah son of Jehoiada did these things, so he had a reputation like the three mighty men. ²⁵ He had a reputation like the Three, but he was not equal to the Three. David put him over his bodyguard.

Warriors of the Army 11:26-47	
Asahel the brother of Joab ²⁶	Joel the brother of Nathan ³⁸
Elhanan son of Dodo from Bethlehem	Mibhar son of Hagri
Shammoth the Harorite ²⁷	Zelek the Ammonite ³⁹
Helez the Pelonite	Naharai the Berothite
Ira son of Ikkesh the Tekoite ²⁸	He was the armor-bearer for Joab
Abiezer the Anathothite	son of Zeruiah.
Sibbecai the Hushathite ²⁹	Ira the Ithrite ⁴⁰
Ilai the Ahohite	Gareb the Ithrite
Maharai the Netophathite ³⁰	Uriah the Hittite ⁴¹
Heled son of Baanah the Netophathite ³¹	Zabad son of Ahlai
Ithai son of Ribai from Gibeah,	Adina son of Shiza the Reubenite ⁴²
a Benjamite	He was a captain of the Reubenites
Benaiah the Pirathonite	and among the Thirty.
Hurai from the ravines of Gaash ³²	Hanan son of Maacah ⁴³
Abiel the Arbathite	Joshaphat the Mithnite
Azmaveth the Baharumite ³³	Uzziah the Ashterathite ⁴⁴
Eliahba the Shaalbonite	Shama and Jeiel
The sons of Hashem the Gizonite ³⁴	the sons of Hotham the Aroerite
Jonathan son of Shagee the Hararite	Jediael son of Shimri and his brother
Ahiam son of Sacar the Hararite ³⁵	Joha the Tizite ⁴⁵
Eliphal son of Ur	Eliel the Mahavite ⁴⁶
Hepher the Mekerathite ³⁶	Jeribai and Joshaviah the sons of Elnaam
Ahijah the Pelonite	Ithmah the Moabite
Hezro the Carmelite ³⁷	Eliel
Naarai son of Ezbai	Obed and Jaasiel the Mezobaite ⁴⁷

---

a The Hebrew is unclear.
b Literally, "five cubits."

Those Who Joined David at Ziklag

David's Key Supporters [12:1-38]

[1] These were the ones who went to David at Ziklag when he was still exiled from Saul son of Kish. They were among the warriors who helped him in battle. [2] They were armed with bows and arrows and were able to *shoot* arrows or *sling* stones with either the right hand or the left. They were Benjamites, kinsmen of Saul.

Ahiezer, their leader, son of Shemaah the Gibeathite [3]	Jozabad the Gederathite
Joash son of Shemaah the Gibeathite	Eluzai [5]
Jeziel son of Azmaveth	Jerimoth
Pelet son of Azmaveth	Bealiah
Beracah	Shemariah
Jehu the Anathothite	Shephatiah the Haruphite
Ishmaiah the Gibeonite [4]	Elkanah [6]
A mighty man of the thirty *mighty men,* and even over them	Isshiah
	Azarel
Jeremiah	Joezer the Korahite
Jahaziel	Jashobeam the Korahite
Johanan	Joelah son of Jeroham from Gedor [7]
	Zebadiah son of Jeroham from Gedor

Gadites

[8] These Gadites went over to David at his stronghold in the wilderness. *They were* warriors, battle-hardened men, lined up with large shields and lances. Their faces were like the faces of lions, and they were as swift as gazelles on the mountains. [14] These Gadites were the elite of the army.[a] The least *of them* was a match for a hundred, and the greatest *of them* was a match for a thousand. [15] These were the ones who crossed the Jordan in the first month *of spring* when it was flooding over all its banks. They routed every single *enemy* in the valleys, from east to west.

Person	Position
Ezer [9]	Chief
Obadiah	Second-in-command
Eliab	Third
Mishmannah [10]	Fourth
Jeremiah	Fifth
Attai [11]	Sixth
Eliel	Seventh
Johanan [12]	Eighth
Elzabad	Ninth
Jeremiah [13]	Tenth
Macbannai	Eleventh

a   Or "were commanders of the army."

Benjamites

[16] Some Benjamites and Judahites came to David in his fortress. [17] David went out to meet them and answered them, saying, "If you have come to me in peace and to help me, my heart will be united with yours. But if you *have come to* betray me to my enemies when there's no violence in my hands, may the God of our ancestors see *it* and punish *you*."

[18] Then the Spirit came upon[a] Amasai, leader of the Thirty, *and he said,*

"We are for you, David!

We are with you, son of Jesse!

Peace, peace to you, and peace to your helper,

for your God is your helper!"

Then David received them and made them leaders of his raiding bands.

Manassites

[19] Some Manassites defected *from Saul* to David when he set out with the Philistines to fight against Saul. However, David's men did not help the Philistines, because, after consultation, the lords of the Philistines sent him away, saying, "*It will cost* our heads if David deserts back to his master Saul." [20] When David went to Ziklag, these Manassite captains of thousands defected to him:

Adnah	Michael
Jozabad	Jozabad (*a second Jozabad*)
Jediael	Elihu
	Zillethai

[21] They helped David against raiding bands, for they were all warriors. They became commanders in the army.

---

a   Literally, "clothed."

David's Troops 12:22-37	
Tribe	**Armed Troops**

22 At that time men were coming day by day to David to help him until they were a great camp, like the army of God. 23 This is the number of troops equipped for battle who came to David at Hebron to turn the kingdom of Saul over to him, according to the word of the LORD.

Tribe	Armed Troops
Judah 24	6,800 who carried large shields and spears, equipped for battle
Simeon 25	7,100 brave warriors
Levi 26	4,600, *including* 27 Jehoiada, a leader of the house of Aaron with 3,700 of his men 28 Zadok, a brave young man, with twenty-two officers
Benjamin 29	3,000 of Saul's relatives, most of whom had remained loyal to Saul until that time
Ephraim 30	20,800 warriors, men who brought renown to their families
Manasseh, half-tribe of 31	18,000, marked by name to come and make David king
Issachar 32	200 chiefs with the rest of their relatives under their orders. They were men who had knowledge and understanding of the times, who knew what Israel should do.
Zebulun 33	50,000 went out to war, arrayed for battle with all their equipment. Determined*a* men.
Naphtali 34	1,000 chiefs 37,000 soldiers armed with large shields and spears
Dan 35	28,600 arrayed for battle
Asher 36	40,000 who went out and prepared themselves for battle
Reuben, Gad, half-tribe of Manasseh 37	120,000 from the other side of the Jordan, armed with all *kinds of* weapons for war
Total	*337,100 plus Issachar's soldiers*

38 All these warriors, who could array themselves for battle, came to Hebron completely committed*b* to make David king over all Israel. All the remaining Israelites were also united to make David king. 39 They were there with David for three days, eating and drinking, for their relatives had supplied *provisions for* them. 40 Even neighbors from as far away as Issachar, Zebulun, and Naphtali were bringing food on donkeys, camels, mules, and oxen—an abundance of flour, fig cakes, raisin cakes, wine, oil, beef, and lamb in abundance—for there was joy in Israel.

---

a   Or "*men* of truth." Literally, "not double-hearted."
b   Literally, "with a whole heart" or "with a perfect heart."

The Ark Moved to Obed-Edom's House

[1] David conferred with the commanders of thousands and hundreds, all the leaders.
[2] Then he said to the assembly of Israel, "If it *seems* good to you and it has come
from the LORD our God, let us send messengers everywhere—to our relatives who are
remaining in all the lands of Israel and to all the priests and Levites in their towns
and pasturelands—that they may meet[a] with us. [3] Let us bring back the ark of our
God to us, for we did not inquire of it in Saul's days." [4] All the assembly said to do it,
for the idea was right in the eyes of all the people.

[5] David brought together all Israel, from the Shihor River of Egypt to Lebo
Hamath, to bring the ark of God from Kiriath Jearim. [6] David and all Israel went up
to Baalah (that is, Kiriath Jearim), which is in Judah, to bring the ark of God up from
there—*the ark* that is called by the name of the LORD, who sits enthroned above the
cherubim. [7] They mounted the ark of God on a new cart from the house of Abinadab,
and Uzzah and Ahio drove it.

[8] David and all Israel were rejoicing before God with all their might with songs,
harps, lyres, tambourines, cymbals, and trumpets. [9] When they arrived at the
threshing floor of Kidon, Uzzah reached out his hand to grasp the ark because the
oxen had stumbled. [10] The LORD was angry with[b] Uzzah, and he struck him because
he reached out his hand to the ark. He died there before God.[c] [11] David became angry
over the LORD's outburst against Uzzah, and he called that place Perez Uzzah (*i.e.,*
Outbreak Against Uzzah). *It is called that* to this day.

[12] David feared God that day and said, "How can I bring the ark of God *home*
to me?" [13] So David did not take the ark with him into the City of David. Instead, he
turned aside to the house of Obed-Edom the Gittite. [14] The ark of God stayed with
Obed-Edom's family at his house for three months. The LORD blessed Obed-Edom's
house and everything in it.

David's Palace

[1] Hiram king of Tyre sent messengers to David with cedar logs, stonemasons, and
carpenters to build his palace. [2] David knew that the LORD had established him as king
over Israel and that his kingdom was highly exalted on behalf of his people Israel.
[3] David married more women in Jerusalem and fathered more sons and daughters.

David's Children Born in Jerusalem 14:4–7			
Shammua [4]	Solomon	Elpelet	Japhia
Shobab	Ibhar [5]	Nogah [6]	Elishama [7]
Nathan	Elishua	Nepheg	Beeliada
			Eliphelet

---

a Literally, "be gathered to us."
b Literally, "The anger of the LORD burned against."
c See 1 Chronicles 15:13 for an explanation of this act of God.

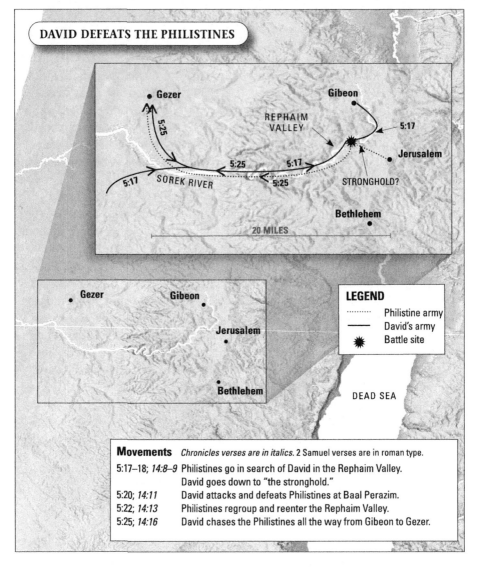

DAVID DEFEATS THE PHILISTINES

REPHAIM VALLEY

Gezer

5:25

Gibeon

5:17

Jerusalem

5:25

5:17

5:17

SOREK RIVER

5:25

STRONGHOLD?

Bethlehem

20 MILES

Gezer

Gibeon

Jerusalem

Bethlehem

DEAD SEA

LEGEND

.... Philistine army

—— David's army

✳ Battle site

Movements *Chronicles verses are in italics.* 2 Samuel verses are in roman type.

5:17–18; *14:8–9*	Philistines go in search of David in the Rephaim Valley. David goes down to "the stronghold."
5:20; *14:11*	David attacks and defeats Philistines at Baal Perazim.
5:22; *14:13*	Philistines regroup and reenter the Rephaim Valley.
5:25; *14:16*	David chases the Philistines all the way from Gibeon to Gezer.

David Defeats the Philistines

[8] When the Philistines heard that David had been anointed king over Israel, all the Philistine *army* went up to search for David. But David heard *about it* and went out before them *to fight.* [9] Now the Philistines had raided the Valley of Rephaim. [10] David asked God, "Should I go up against the Philistines? Will you put them in my hand?"

The LORD said to him, "Go up and I will put them in your hand."

[11] So they went up at Baal Perazim, and David defeated them there. David said, "By my hand God has broken out like a flood against my enemies." Therefore they named that place Baal-Perazim (*i.e.,* God Who Breaks Out). [12] The Philistines abandoned their gods there, and David commanded that they be burned in the fire.

[13] The Philistines raided the valley again. [14] David asked God *for guidance* again, and God said to him, "Do not go up after them. Circle around them and attack them

in front of the balsam trees. [15] When you hear the sound of marching in the tree tops, then move out to fight, for God will have gone out ahead of you to strike down the Philistine army." [16] David did as God had commanded him. He struck down the Philistine army *all the way* from Gibeon to Gezer. [17] So the name of David went out to all the lands, and the LORD made all the nations dread him.

The Ark Brought to Jerusalem

[1] David built houses for himself in the City of David, and he prepared a place for the ark of God and pitched a tent for it. [2] Then David said, "No one is to carry the ark of God except for the Levites, for the LORD chose them to carry the ark of the LORD and to minister to him forever." [3] David assembled all Israel in Jerusalem to bring the ark of the LORD up to the place he had prepared for it. [4] He assembled the descendants of Aaron and the Levites.

Descendants of Aaron and the Levites [15:5-10]		
Clan	**Chief**	**Relatives**
Kohath [5]	Uriel	120
Merari [6]	Asaiah	220
Gershon [7]	Joel	130
Elizaphan [8]	Shemaiah	200
Hebron [9]	Eliel	80
Uzziel [10]	Amminadab	112

Heads of the Levite Households [15:11-16]		
[11] David called		
The priests	Zadok	Abiathar
The *other* Levites	Uriel	Shemaiah
	Asaiah	Eliel
	Joel	Amminadab

[12] David said to them, "You are the heads of the families[a] of the Levites. Consecrate yourselves and your brothers and then bring the ark of the LORD, the God of Israel, up to the place I have established for it. [13] The LORD our God broke out against us, because you did not *carry* it the first time and because we did not consult his instructions." [14] So the priests and Levites consecrated themselves in order to bring up the ark of the LORD, the God of Israel. [15] The Levites carried the ark of God with the poles on their shoulders, just as Moses commanded by the word of the LORD. [16] Then David ordered the leaders of the Levites to station their brothers the singers, along with *those with* musical instruments—harps, lyres, and cymbals—to make sounds of joy.

---

a Literally, "the fathers."

Levite Musician Positions 15:17-24		
Position	**Person**	**Comment**
First tier	[17] Heman son of Joel	
	Asaph son of Berekiah	From Heman's relatives
	Ethan son of Kushaiah	From the descendants of their relative Merari
Second tier	[18] Their relatives: Zechariah[a] Benaiah Jaaziel Maaseiah Shemiramoth Mattithiah Jehiel Eliphelehu Unni Mikneiah Eliab Obed-Edom Jeiel	The gatekeepers
Bronze cymbal players [19]	Heman Asaph Ethan	
Lyre players [20]	Zechariah Unni Aziel Eliab Shemiramoth Maaseiah Jehiel Benaiah	*Playing* according to alamoth[b]
Harpists [21]	Mattithiah Obed-Edom Eliphelehu Jeiel Mikneiah Azaziah	Directing according to sheminith[c]
Choirmaster [22]	Kenaniah, the chief Levite	He instructed in singing because he was skilled at it.
Gatekeepers for the ark [23]	Berekia Obed-Edom [24b] Elkanah Jehiah	
Trumpeters before the ark of God [24a]	Shebaniah Amasai Joshaphat Zechariah Nethanel Benaiah Eliezer	The priests

[25] David, the elders of Israel, and the commanders of thousands went to bring the ark of the covenant of the LORD up from the house of Obed-Edom with rejoicing. [26] They sacrificed seven bulls and seven rams because God helped the Levites carry the ark of the covenant of the LORD. [27] David was clothed in a robe of fine fabric, as were all the Levites who were carrying the ark and the singers, as well as Kenaniah the leader of the singers.[d] David was *also* wearing a linen ephod. [28] All Israel was bringing up the ark of the covenant of the LORD with shouts of joy and sounds of the horn,

a   From some Hebrew manuscripts and the Septuagint; Masoretic text includes "son" or the name "Ben" after Zechariah.
b   An unknown musical term.
c   An unknown musical term.
d   From the Septuagint; Masoretic text: "Kenaniah the leader of the carriers who were singers."

trumpets, cymbals, and the playing of harps and lyres. ²⁹ So the ark of the covenant of the Lᴏʀᴅ entered the City of David. But Michal the daughter of Saul looked down from the window and saw King David dancing and celebrating, and she despised him in her heart. ¹⁶:¹ᵃ They brought in the ark of God and placed it in the tent that David had pitched for it.

1 Chronicles 16

Offerings and Celebration

¹ᵇ Then they offered burnt offerings and fellowship offerings before God. ² When David finished offering burnt offerings and fellowship offerings, he blessed the people in the name of the Lᴏʀᴅ. ³ Then he distributed to each Israelite man and woman a loaf of bread, a cake of dates, and a cake of raisins. ⁴ He placed some of the Levites before the ark of the Lᴏʀᴅ to serve, to bring to remembrance *the deeds of the Lᴏʀᴅ,* and to thank and praise the Lᴏʀᴅ, the God of Israel.

⁵ Asaph was the head.

Next in rank was Zechariah, *then* Jeiel, Shemiramoth, Jehiel, Mattithiah, Eliab, Benaiah, Obed-Edom, and Jeiel, who played harps and lyres, and Asaph, who played cymbals.

⁶ Benaiah and Jahaziel were the priests who blew the trumpets regularly before the ark of the covenant of God.

David's Psalm of Thanksgiving

⁷ On that day David first assigned Asaph and his relatives to give thanks to the Lᴏʀᴅ *with this song:*

Make Known the Deeds of the Lord

⁸ O give thanks to the Lᴏʀᴅ;
Call upon his name;
Make his deeds known among the people,
⁹ Sing to him; sing praises to him;
Tell of all his wondrous works;
¹⁰ Glory in his holy name;
Let the hearts of those who seek the Lᴏʀᴅ rejoice.

¹¹ Seek the Lᴏʀᴅ;
Seek his strength;
Seek his face continually.
¹² Remember the marvelous works he has done,
His wonders and the judgments *spoken* by his mouth.

Consider How God Remembers His Covenant

¹³ O you descendants of his servant Israel,
O you descendants of Jacob, his chosen ones,
¹⁴ He is the Lᴏʀᴅ our God;
His judgments are throughout the earth.

¹⁵ He forever remembers his covenant,
That is,
The words he commanded to a thousand generations—
¹⁶ The *covenant* he made with Abraham and
His oath to Isaac,
¹⁷ Which he confirmed as a decree to Jacob and as an everlasting
covenant to Israel,
¹⁸ When he said, "I will give you the land of Canaan as your
portion for an inheritance";
¹⁹ When they were few in number, few indeed, and strangers in it;
²⁰ When they wandered from nation to nation, from *one* kingdom
to another.^{*a*}
²¹ He allowed no man to oppress them.
He *even* rebuked kings for their sakes,
²² Saying, "Do not touch my anointed ones or harm my prophets."

Praise the Lord

²³ Sing to the LORD, all the earth;
Proclaim his salvation day after day.
²⁴ Declare his glory among the pagan nations;
Declare his wonders among all people *like this*:
²⁵ "The LORD is great and greatly to be praised;
He is to be feared above all gods.
²⁶ For all the gods of *other* people are *only* idols,
But the LORD made the heavens.
²⁷ Splendor and majesty are before him;
Strength and beauty are in his *dwelling* place."

²⁸ Give credit to the LORD, you families of nations;
Recognize the LORD's glory and strength;
²⁹ Give to the LORD the glory due his name.
Bring an offering and come before him;
Worship the LORD in the splendor of his holiness.
³⁰ Tremble before him, all the earth.
Indeed, the world stands firm *by his power*; it will not be moved.

³¹ Let the heavens be glad;
Let the earth rejoice;
³² Let the sea and everything in it roar *with joy*;
Let the field and everything in it sing with joy.
³³ Then all the trees of the forest will rejoice before the LORD,
For he is coming to judge the earth.

³⁴ Give thanks to the LORD,
For he is good,
For his lovingkindness endures forever.

---

a   Literally, "to another people."

35 Then say,

"Save us, O God of our salvation;
Gather and rescue us from the pagan nations
    To give thanks to your holy name and
    To glory in your praise."
36 Blessed be the LORD, the God of Israel, from everlasting to everlasting!
And all the people said, "Amen."
Hallelujah!

Ministers and Guardians of the Ark 16:37–43

37 David left these men to serve 39b before the tabernacle of the LORD on the high place at Gibeon:

Position	Person	Duties
Ministers 37b	Asaph and his relatives Obed-Edom and his sixty-eight relatives 38a	To minister before the ark continually, as each day required*a*
Gatekeepers 38b	Obed-Edom son of Jeduthun*b* and Hosah 42b Jeduthun's sons were *also* at the gate.	
Priests 39a	Zadok and his brother priests	40 To offer burnt offerings to the LORD continually on the altar for burnt offerings, morning and evening, according to all that was written in the Law of the LORD, which he commanded Israel
Musicians 41	Heman and Jeduthun and the rest of those chosen	Designated by name to give thanks to the LORD, for his love is forever. 42a Heman and Jeduthun had trumpets, cymbals, and other musical instruments with them for making God's praise resound.

43 Then everyone returned to their home, and David returned to bless his household.

1 Chronicles **17**

David's Promise to Build a House for God

1 When David was settled in at his palace, he said to Nathan the prophet, "Look, I am living in a house *made* of cedar while the ark of the covenant of the LORD is in a tent!"*c*
2 Nathan said to David, "Do whatever is in your heart, for God is with you."

---

a Literally, "for the matter of a day in its day."
b Whether this is the same Obed-Edom as the one directly above is unclear.
c Literally, "under curtains."

³ But that night the word of God came to Nathan, ⁴ "Go tell my servant David, 'The Lord says this: You will not build a house for me to dwell in, ⁵ for I have not dwelt in a house from the day I brought Israel up *from Egypt* until today. I went from campsite to campsite, from *one* dwelling place to *another*. ⁶ Wherever I have visited*ᵃ* in all Israel, did I ever say to one of the judges, whom I commanded to shepherd my people, "Why have you not built a house of cedar for me?" '

⁷ "Now tell all this to David my servant:

'The Lord of Armies says this: I took you from the pasture, from following the flock, to become the ruler over my people Israel. ⁸ I have been with you everywhere you went, and I mowed down all your enemies before you. I will give you a reputation like those of the great *kings* on the earth. ⁹ I will appoint a place for my people Israel and plant them, so they may live in their own place and not be disturbed anymore. Wicked people will no longer oppress them like in the past, ¹⁰ in the days when I appointed judges over my people Israel. I will subdue all your enemies.

"'I declare to you that the Lord will build a family*ᵇ* for you. ¹¹ When your days are completed and you lie down with your fathers, I will raise up a descendant after you, one of your sons, and I will establish his kingdom. ¹² He will build a temple for me, and I will establish his throne forever. ¹³ I will be like a father to him, and he will be a son to me. I will never remove my loyal love from him like I removed *it* from Saul, who was before you. ¹⁴ I will set him over my house and over my kingdom forever, and his throne will be secure forever.' "

¹⁵ Nathan related all these words and all this vision to David.

¹⁶ Then David went in and sat before the Lord and said,

"Who am I, Lord God, and who is my family that you have brought me this far? ¹⁷ And while this was a small thing in your eyes, O God, you have made promises about the future of the family of your servant. You have looked upon me in my human condition and exalted me, O Lord God.*ᶜ* ¹⁸ What more can David say to you, for you have glorified your servant, and you have known him. ¹⁹ O Lord, according to your heart you have done all these great things for the sake of your servant and made known all these great promises.*ᵈ*

²⁰ "O Lord, there is none like you, and there is no God beside you, *none* like we have heard with our ears. ²¹ And who is like your people Israel, a unique people on the earth whom God went with to redeem them for himself, to make a name for himself, *performing* awesome works by driving out nations before your people, whom you redeemed from Egypt? ²² You made your people Israel to be a people for yourself forever, and you, O Lord, have become their God.

²³ "And now, O Lord, may the word that you have spoken concerning your servant and his family be made firm forever. Do just as you said. ²⁴ May your

---

a   Literally, "In all wherever I have walked."
b   Literally, "house." And verses 16, 23–27.
c   From the Septuagint; the Masoretic text is uncertain.
d   Literally, "great things."

name be firm and be magnified forever, *that it may be said,* 'The Lord of Armies is the God of Israel, Israel's God!' May the family of your servant David be established before you. ²⁵ For you are my God; you have revealed to*ᵃ* your servant that you will build his family *dynasty.* Therefore your servant has found *courage* to pray to you.

²⁶ "Now O Lord, you *alone* are God! You have promised this good thing to your servant. ²⁷ Now may it please you to bless your servant's family so it will continue to be before you always. It is blessed forever because you, O Lord, have blessed it."

David Secures His Kingdom

¹ After all this, David attacked the Philistines and soundly defeated*ᵇ* them. He took Gath and its surrounding villages from the hand of the Philistines;
² defeated Moab,
and they became David's servants and brought him tribute. ³ David defeated Hadadezer king of Zobah in Hamath
when he went to establish his rule at the Euphrates River. ⁴ David captured one thousand chariots, seven thousand horsemen, and twenty thousand infantry from him. He hamstrung all but one hundred of *his enemies'* chariot horses. ⁵ He
slew twenty-two thousand Arameans of Damascus when they came to help Hadadezer king of Zobah.
⁶ David installed *garrisons* in Syrian Damascus, and the Arameans brought tribute and became his servants.
The Lord gave David victory wherever he went. ⁷ David
took the golden shields, which were carried by Hadadezer's servants, and brought them to Jerusalem. ⁸ David
took a huge quantity of bronze from Hadadezer's cities, Tebah and Cun. Solomon made the bronze Sea, pillars, and utensils with it.

⁹ Tou king of Hamath heard that David had destroyed the whole army of Hadadezer king of Zobah. ¹⁰ So he sent Hadoram his son to King David, to greet him and bless him, because he had fought against Hadadezer and defeated him (for Hadadezer had been at war with Tou). And *Hadoram brought* all kinds of articles of gold and silver and bronze. ¹¹ King David dedicated these to the Lord along with all the silver and gold he had taken from the *enemy* peoples: the Edomites, Moabites, Ammonites, Philistines, and Amalekites.

¹² Abishai son of Zeruiah struck down eighteen thousand Edomites in the Valley of Salt. ¹³ He placed garrisons in Edom, and the Edomites became servants to David. The Lord gave victory to David wherever he went. ¹⁴ David reigned over all Israel, doing justice and righteousness for all the people.

---

a   Literally, "you have opened the ear of."
b   Or "humbled." See map at 2 Samuel 5.

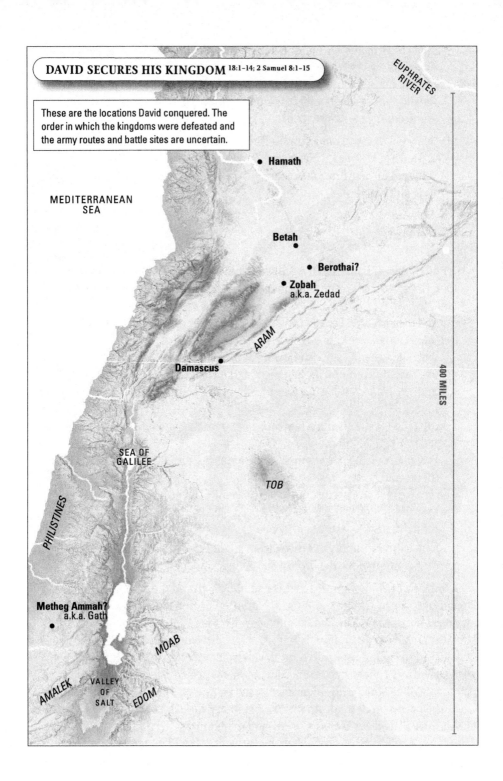

DAVID SECURES HIS KINGDOM 18:1-14; 2 Samuel 8:1-15

These are the locations David conquered. The order in which the kingdoms were defeated and the army routes and battle sites are uncertain.

EUPHRATES RIVER

Hamath

MEDITERRANEAN SEA

Betah

Berothai?

Zobah
a.k.a. Zedad

ARAM

Damascus

400 MILES

SEA OF GALILEE

TOB

PHILISTINES

Metheg Ammah?
a.k.a. Gath

MOAB

AMALEK VALLEY OF SALT EDOM

David's Staff 18:15-17	
Army commander[a] 15	Joab son of Zeruiah
Royal secretary	Jehoshaphat son of Ahilud
Priests 16	Zadok son of Ahitub Ahimelech son of Abiathar
Scribe	Shavsha
Over the *elite troops* (i.e., the Kerethites and Pelethites) 17	Benaiah son of Jehoiada
Close advisors to the king[b]	David's sons

1 Chronicles **19**

Victory over Ammon and Aram

1 After these things, the king of the Ammonites died, and his son reigned in his place. 2 David said, "I will show kindness to Hanun the son of Nahash because his father dealt kindly with me." So David sent messengers with condolences concerning his father. David's servants entered the land of the Ammonites.

3 But the princes of the Ammonites said to Hanun, *"Do you think* David is honoring your father before your eyes by sending you comforters? Haven't they come to explore, overthrow, and spy out the land? *That is why* his servants are coming to you." 4 Hanun seized David's servants, shaved them, cut off their clothes halfway down at their buttocks, and sent them away.

5 *Some people* reported to David about the men. David sent messengers to them, for the men were terribly humiliated. The king said, "Stay at Jericho until your beards have grown back, then come home." 6 When the Ammonites realized that they had made themselves repulsive to David, Hanun and the Ammonites sent 75,000 pounds[c] of silver to hire chariots and horsemen from Aram Naharaim, Aram Maacah, and Zobah. 7 They hired 32,000 chariots, the king of Maacah, and his army. They came and encamped at Medeba, while the Ammonites mustered themselves from their cities and came *ready* for battle.

8 David heard *about this* and sent Joab with the entire army of fighting men. 9 The Ammonites came out and formed battle lines at the city gate, while the kings went by themselves in the field. 10 Joab saw that he was outflanked,[d] so he chose some of the best in Israel and positioned them against the Arameans. 11 He put the remaining men under the hand of his brother Abishai, positioning them against the Ammonites. 12 And he said, "If the Arameans are too strong for me, come to my aid. If the Ammonites are too strong for you, I will come to yours. 13 Be strong and courageous for our people's sake and for the cities of our God, and may the LORD do what is good in his eyes."

---

a Literally, "Over the army."
b Literally, "First at the hand of the king."
c Literally, "1,000 talents"
d Literally, "that the face of the battle was to him before and behind."

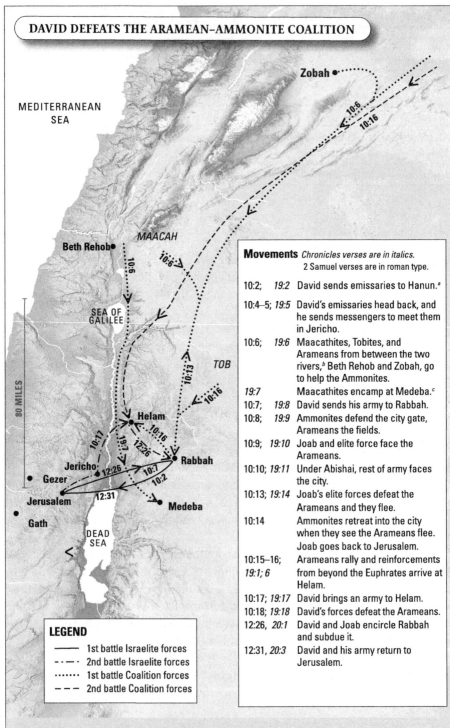

DAVID DEFEATS THE ARAMEAN-AMMONITE COALITION

Zobah

MEDITERRANEAN SEA

10:5
10:16

Beth Rehob

MAACAH

10:6
10:6

SEA OF GALILEE

10:13

TOB

80 MILES

10:16

Helam

10:17
19:7
12:26
10:16

Jericho

Gezer

12:26

Rabbah

10:7
10:2

Jerusalem

12:31

Medeba

Gath

DEAD SEA

Movements *Chronicles verses are in italics.*
2 Samuel verses are in roman type.

10:2;	*19:2*	David sends emissaries to Hanun.[a]
10:4–5;	*19:5*	David's emissaries head back, and he sends messengers to meet them in Jericho.
10:6;	*19:6*	Maacathites, Tobites, and Arameans from between the two rivers,[b] Beth Rehob and Zobah, go to help the Ammonites.
	19:7	Maacathites encamp at Medeba.[c]
10:7;	*19:8*	David sends his army to Rabbah.
10:8;	*19:9*	Ammonites defend the city gate, Arameans the fields.
10:9;	*19:10*	Joab and elite force face the Arameans.
10:10;	*19:11*	Under Abishai, rest of army faces the city.
10:13;	*19:14*	Joab's elite forces defeat the Arameans and they flee.
10:14		Ammonites retreat into the city when they see the Arameans flee. Joab goes back to Jerusalem.
10:15–16;		Arameans rally and reinforcements
19:1; 6		from beyond the Euphrates arrive at Helam.
10:17;	*19:17*	David brings an army to Helam.
10:18;	*19:18*	David's forces defeat the Arameans.
12:26,	*20:1*	David and Joab encircle Rabbah and subdue it.
12:31,	*20:3*	David and his army return to Jerusalem.

LEGEND

——— 1st battle Israelite forces
— · — · 2nd battle Israelite forces
· · · · · · 1st battle Coalition forces
— — — 2nd battle Coalition forces

a Since Rabbah was the chief Ammonite city, the messengers are shown as going there.
b "Cities between the two rivers": Hebrew: *Aram Naharaim.* The land between the Tigris and Euphrates (i.e., Mesopotamia).
c Since Medeba is a Moabite city, the map assumes the ensuing battle was at Rabbah, an Ammonite city.

¹⁴ So Joab and the troops with him engaged the Arameans in battle, and they fled before him. ¹⁵ The Ammonites saw that the Arameans fled, so they fled before Joab's brother Abishai and retreated into the city. And Joab went back to Jerusalem.

¹⁶ When the Arameans saw that they were beaten by Israel, they sent messengers to bring out the Arameans who were beyond the *Euphrates* River. Shophach, commander of Hadadezer's army, led them. ¹⁷ David was told about this, so he mustered all Israel, crossed the Jordan River, and went *to fight* them. When David formed battle lines opposite them, the Aramean forces fought with him. ¹⁸ The Arameans fled before Israel. David slew seven thousand Aramean charioteers and forty thousand infantrymen, and he killed Shophach, the commander of the army. ¹⁹ When the servants of Hadadezer saw that they were beaten by Israel, they surrendered to David and became his subjects. The Arameans were never willing to help the Ammonites again.

1 Chronicles 20

Victory over the Ammonites and the Philistines

¹ In the spring,ᵃ the time when kings go out *to fight,* Joab led the army and ravaged the land of Ammon. He set siege to Rabbah while David remained in Jerusalem. Joab defeated Rabbah and demolished it. ² David took the crown off their king's head, and it was *placed* on his own head. Its weight was determined to be seventy-five poundsᵇ of gold, and it had a precious stone in it. He brought out a huge amount of plunder from the city. ³ He brought out the people who were in it and made them work with saws, iron picks, and axes. David did this to all the Ammonite towns. Then David and all the army returned to Jerusalem.

⁴ And war broke out again with the Philistines at Gezer. Then Sibbecai the Hushathite killed Sippai, a descendant of the Rephaim *giants,* and the Philistines were subdued. ⁵ And there was war with the Philistines again, and Elhanan son of Jair killed Lahmi, the brother of Goliath the Gittite, whose spear shaft was like the beam of a weaver's *loom.*

⁶ There was another battle at Gath. There was a man of *huge* stature who had six fingers on each hand and six toes on each foot, twenty-four in all. He was also a descendant of Rapha. ⁷ He insulted Israel, and Jonathan son of David's brother Shimeah killed him. ⁸ They were the descendants of Rapha in Gath. They fell by the hand of David and his servants.

1 Chronicles 21

David's Census Brings a Plague

¹ Then Satan stood up against Israel, and he incited David to take a census of Israel. ² So David said to Joab and the army commanders, "Go and count *the people of* Israel from Beersheba to Dan. Bring *the tally* to me that I may know their number."

---

a   Or "At the turn of the year." The Jewish year begins within fifteen days of the spring equinox.
b   Literally, "a talent."

³ Joab said, "May the LORD increase the army a hundred times over! Doesn't my lord the king rule over them all as his servants? Why seek this *knowledge,* my lord? Why be a cause of guilt to Israel?"

⁴ The king's order, however, prevailed over Joab so he went throughout all Israel. Then he returned to Jerusalem. ⁵ Joab gave the number of the census of the army to David. All Israel numbered 1,100,000 men who could draw the sword, and Judah numbered 470,000 men who could draw the sword ⁶ But Joab did not count the Levites and Benjamites among them, because the king's command was repugnant to him. ⁷ David did evil in the eyes of God in this matter, so he struck Israel.

⁸ David said to God, "I sinned terribly when I did this thing. Now please remove your servant's guilt, for I behaved extremely foolishly."

⁹ The LORD spoke to Gad, David's seer, and said, ¹⁰ "Go and tell David: 'The LORD says this: I am offering^a three *options* for you. Choose one of them for yourself, and I will do it for you.'"

¹¹ So Gad went to David and said to him,

"The LORD says this: 'Choose for yourself:

¹² three years of famine, or

three months of devastation before your foes with the sword of your enemies overtaking you, or

three days of the sword of the LORD, a plague in the land—the angel of the LORD slaughtering in all the borders of Israel!'

Now decide; what word shall I take back to the one who sent me?"

¹³ David said to Gad, "I am in terrible straits. Please let me fall into the hand of the LORD, for his mercy is very great. Let me not fall into the hands of men."

¹⁴ So the LORD sent a plague upon Israel, and seventy thousand Israelites fell *dead.* ¹⁵ God sent the angel to Jerusalem to massacre *its inhabitants. While* he was slaughtering, the LORD saw and reconsidered the disaster and said to the destroying angel, "Enough now! Withdraw your hand." The angel of the LORD was standing at the threshing floor of Araunah the Jebusite.

¹⁶ David raised his eyes and saw the angel of the LORD standing between earth and heaven with his drawn sword in his hand stretched out over Jerusalem. Then David and the elders, wearing sackcloth, fell on their faces.

¹⁷ David said to God, "Wasn't it I who ordered the numbering of the people? It was I who sinned and did this evil. But these sheep, what have they done? O LORD my God, let your hand be against me and my father's house. Don't let the plague be upon your people."

¹⁸ The angel of the LORD told Gad to tell David that he should go up and erect an altar to the LORD on the threshing floor of Araunah the Jebusite. ¹⁹ So David went up in *obedience to* Gad's word that he spoke in the name of the LORD.

²⁰ Now Araunah was threshing wheat. He turned and saw the angel, and his four sons who were with him hid themselves. ²¹ David approached Araunah, and Araunah looked and saw David. He left his threshing floor and bowed down before

---

a   Literally, "I am stretching out."

David with his face to the ground. ²² David said to Araunah, "Give me the site of your threshing floor, that I may build an altar to the Lord on it. I will pay the full price for it. Then the plague will be withdrawn from the people."

²³ Araunah replied, "Take it, and may my lord the king do what is good in his eyes. Look, I am giving the bull for the burnt offering, the threshing sledges for wood, and wheat for the grain offering; I am giving it all."

²⁴ But King David said to Araunah, "No, I insist on buying it for the full price in silver, for I will not take what is yours and give it to*a* the Lord; for I will not offer a burnt offering that costs me nothing." ²⁵ David paid Araunah fifteen pounds*b* of gold for the place.

²⁶ Then David built an altar to the Lord there and sacrificed burnt offerings and fellowship offerings. He called on the Lord, and he answered him with fire from heaven upon the altar for burnt offerings. ²⁷ The Lord commanded the angel, and he put his sword back in its sheath. ²⁸ At that time, when David saw that the Lord had answered him at Araunah the Jebusite's threshing floor, he sacrificed there— ²⁹ for the tabernacle of the Lord that Moses had made in the wilderness and the altar for burnt offerings were on the high place in Gibeon at that time. ³⁰ David was not able to come before it to inquire of God, for he was terrified of the sword of the angel of the Lord. ²²:¹ David said, "Here will be the temple of the Lord, the only God, and here will be the altar for burnt offerings in Israel."

1 Chronicles 22

David's Instructions to Solomon

² David gave orders that the foreigners in the land of Israel be rounded up and put to work*c* as stonecutters to make dressed stone for building the temple of God. ³ David provided huge quantities of iron for nails for the doors of the gates and more bronze than could be weighed for the braces, ⁴ plus cedar logs beyond counting. The people of Sidon and Tyre brought many logs to David. ⁵ David said, "My son Solomon is young and indecisive.*d* The temple to be built for the Lord should be amazingly great, of the highest reputation, and more beautiful *than any* in all the nations. I will set it up*e* for him." So David made many preparations before his death.

⁶ He called to his son Solomon and commanded him to build a temple for the Lord, the God of Israel. ⁷ David said to Solomon,

"My son, it was in my heart to build a temple for the name of the Lord my God. ⁸ But the word of the Lord came to me, saying, 'You have spilled so much blood and have waged great wars. You are not to build a temple for my name, because you have spilled so much blood on the earth before my face. ⁹ But a son will be born to you. He will be a peaceful man, for I will give him rest from all his enemies everywhere. Solomon will be his name, and I will give Israel peace and quiet in his days. ¹⁰ He will build a temple for my name. He will be my son, and I will be his father. I will establish his royal throne over Israel forever.'

---

a Literally, "is yours for."
b Literally, "600 gold shekels."
c Literally, "be appointed" or "be set."
d Literally, "and tender."
e Literally, "I will establish it" or "prepare it."

¹¹ "Now, my son, may the LORD be with you. May you be successful and build the temple of the LORD your God, just as he said about you. ¹² Only may the LORD give you discretion and insight, so when he puts you in charge over Israel you may keep the Law of the LORD your God. ¹³ Then you will succeed if you continue to observe the statutes and judgments that the LORD commanded for Israel through Moses. Be strong and courageous! Do not be afraid or discouraged. ¹⁴ Be sure—with great pains I have prepared for the temple of the LORD 3,750 tons of gold, 37,500 tons of silver,^a and bronze and iron beyond measure, for they are in great quantity. I have *also* prepared wood and stone, which you must add to. ¹⁵ There are many workmen with you: stonecutters, masons, and carpenters, all of whom are skilled in all kinds of work. ¹⁶ The gold, silver, bronze, and iron are without limit. Now get up and get to work, and may the LORD be with you."

¹⁷ David commanded all the leaders of Israel to help his son Solomon, *saying,*
   ¹⁸ "Isn't the LORD your God with you? Hasn't *he* given you rest on every side? He put the *former* inhabitants of the land in my hand and subdued the land before the LORD and his people. ¹⁹ Now focus^b your heart and soul to seek the LORD your God. Rise up and build the sanctuary of the LORD God, to bring the ark of the covenant of the LORD and the holy articles of God into the house that will be built for the name of the LORD."

23 *1 Chronicles*

Organization of Levite Temple Service

¹ When David was old and full of days, he made his son Solomon king over Israel. ² He gathered the leaders of Israel, the priests, and the Levites. ³ They counted the Levites who were thirty years old or more. They totaled 38,000 men.

Levite Census ^{23:3-5}	
Those thirty years old or more	
Servers in the temple of the LORD ⁴	24,000
Recorders and judges	6,000
Doorkeepers ⁵	4,000
Musicians who praised the LORD with instruments made for giving praise	4,000
Total ³	38,000

---

a   Literally, "one hundred thousand talents" and "a million talents," respectively.
b   Literally, "Now give."

[6] David organized the Levites into divisions according to the lineages of Gershon, Kohath, and Merari.

Gershon

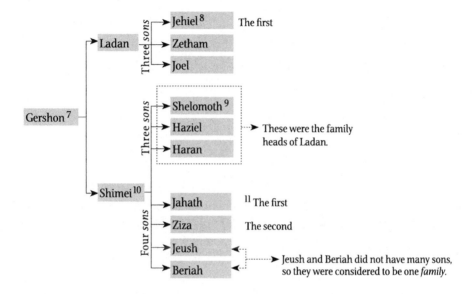

Kohath

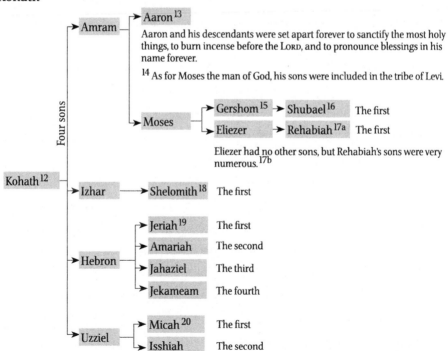

Merari

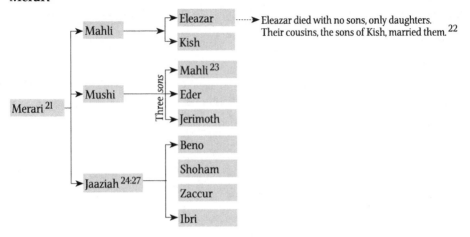

^{24} These were the descendants of Levi according to their families, the family heads according to their registry by name and individual count. From twenty years old or more, they did the service work in the temple of the Lord. ^{25} For David had said, "The Lord God of Israel has given *his people* rest. And he dwells in Jerusalem forever. ^{26} Moreover, regarding the Levites, they will no longer have to carry the tabernacle nor the articles for its service."

^{27} In accordance with the last instructions of David, the Levites were numbered from twenty years old and up. ^{28} Their responsibilities were

to assist^a *the priests*, the descendants of Aaron, and

to serve at the temple of the Lord, in the courts and chambers—*that is*,

purifying all the holy things and

performing the service of the temple of God— ^{29} *assisting with*

the showbread,

the fine flour for the grain offering,

the wafers of unleavened bread,

the baked offering,

the offering mixed with oil, and

all measures of weight and volume,

^{30} standing every morning and evening,

thanking and praising the Lord, ^{31} and

continually before the Lord offering all the burnt offerings to the Lord

on Sabbaths, New Moon *Festivals*, and sacred assemblies in the

number *set* by the ordinance prescribing them.

^{32} They were to keep charge of the meeting tent, the holy *place,* and *to attend to* the priests,^{b} their relatives, for the service of the temple of the Lord.

---

a   Literally, "Their responsibilities were at the hand of."
b   Literally, "the sons of Aaron."

Organization of the Priests and Levites

¹ The descendants of Aaron according to their divisions:

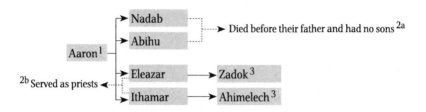

³ Zadok of the sons of Eleazar and Ahimelech of the sons of Ithamar assisted David in organizing *the priests* into divisions according to their appointed ministry tasks. ⁴ More leaders were found among the descendants of Eleazar than among the descendants of Ithamar, so they were organized *accordingly*:
   sixteen family heads from Eleazar's descendants and
   eight *family heads* from Ithamar's descendants.

⁵ They organized them group by group^a by *casting* lots, as there were sanctuary officials and officers of God from the descendants of both Eleazar and Ithamar. ⁶ Shemaiah the Levite scribe, son of Nethanel, recorded the assignments^b in the presence of the king and his officials: Zadok the priest, Ahimelech son of Abiathar, and the family heads of the priests and Levites—one family taken from Eleazar and then one from Ithamar.

Levite Duty Rotation Order 24:7-18		
As determined by casting lots		
1. Jehoiarib⁷	9. Jeshua¹¹	17. Hezir¹⁵
2. Jedaiah	10. Shecaniah	18. Happizzez
3. Harim⁸	11. Eliashib¹²	19. Pethahiah
4. Seorim	12. Jakim	20. Jehezkel¹⁶
5. Malkijah⁹	13. Huppah¹³	21. Jakin¹⁷
6. Mijamin	14. Jeshebeab	22. Gamul
7. Hakkoz¹⁰	15. Bilgah¹⁴	23. Delaiah¹⁸
8. Abijah	16. Immer	24. Maaziah

¹⁹ This was their prescribed order to come to the temple *to carry out the* service of the Lᴏʀᴅ according to the regulations *given* by the hand of their ancestor Aaron the priest, just as the Lᴏʀᴅ God of Israel had commanded him.

a Literally, "these by these."
b Literally, "recorded them."

20a These are the rest of the descendants of Levi. 30b These were the sons of the Levites according to their father's households. 31 They also cast lots according to their families alongside their relatives the priests in the presence of King David, Zadok, Ahimelech, and the family heads of the priests and Levites. The families of the oldest and youngest were treated equally.

Family Head	Sons		Grandsons
Amram 20b	Shubael		Jehdeiah
Rehabiah 21	Isshiah (chief)		
Izhar 22	Shelomoth		Jahath
Hebron 23	Jeriah *1st*	Jahaziel 3rd	
	Amariah 2nd	Jekameam 4th	
Uzziel 24	Micah		Shamir
	Isshiah 25		Zechariah
Merari 26	Mahli		Eleazar, who had no sons 28
	Mushi		Mahli, Eder, Jerimoth 30a
	Jaaziah		Beno, Shoham, Zaccur, Ibri 27
		Father unclear	Kish, whose son was Jerahmeel 29

25 *1 Chronicles*

1 David and the army commanders set aside for service the descendants of Asaph, Heman, and Jeduthun to prophesy with lyres, harps, and cymbals. This is the registry of the men who performed this service.

Family Head/ Supervisor	Musicians		Comments
Asaph 2	Zaccur	Nethaniah	Asaph *himself* prophesied under the king's supervision.
	Joseph	Asarelah	
Jeduthun 3	Gedaliah	Shimei*a*	Under their father Jeduthun's direction, they used the harp to thank and praise the LORD.
	Zeri	Hashabiah	
	Jeshaiah	Mattithiah	
Heman 4	Bukkiah	Joshbekashah	5 All these were the sons of Heman, the king's seer, according to God's promise*b* to exalt him (so God gave him fourteen sons and three daughters).
	Mattaniah	Mallothi	
	Uzziel	Hothir	
	Shubael & Jerimoth	Mahazioth	
	Hananiah		
	Hanani		
	Eliathah		
	Giddalti & Romamti-Ezer		

a From some ancient manuscripts; not in Masoretic text.
b Literally, "in accordance with God's Word."

[6] All these were under the supervision of their fathers when they sang in the temple accompanied by cymbals, harps, and lyres for the service in the temple of the LORD. Asaph, Jeduthun, and Heman were under the supervision of the king. [7] Their number, along with their relatives, all of whom were trained and skillful in music for the LORD, was 288.

Lot Results 25:8-31

[8] All of them, young and old, teacher and student, cast lots together for their duties *Each lot fell to the person below plus* "twelve of each person's sons and relatives."[a]

1. Joseph (for Asaph) [9]
2. Gedaliah
3. Zaccur [10]
4. Izri [11]
5. Nethaniah [12]
6. Bukkiah [13]
7. Jesarelah[b] [14]
8. Jeshaiah [15]
9. Mattaniah [16]
10. Shimei [17]
11. Azarel[c] [18]
12. Hashabiah [19]
13. Shubael [20]
14. Mattithiah [21]
15. Jerimoth [22]
16. Hananiah [23]
17. Joshbekashah [24]
18. Hanani [25]
19. Mallothi [26]
20. Eliathah [27]
21. Hothir [28]
22. Giddalti [29]
23. Mahazioth [30]
24. Romamti-Ezer [31]

Gatekeepers Assigned to Gates by Lot 26:1-12

[12] These divisions of the gatekeepers served under their leaders just as their relatives had, ministering in the temple of the LORD.

Divisions	Family Heads	Sons			
Korahites[1]	Meshelemiah son of Kore, descendant of Asaph	Zechariah[2]	1st	Jathniel	4th
		Jediael	2nd	Elam[3]	5th
		Zebadiah	3rd	Jehohanan	6th
				Eliehoenai	7th
		Meshelemiah's sons and relatives totaled eighteen in all. [9]			
	Obed-Edom[4]	Shemaiah	1st	Nethanel	5th
		Jehozabad	2nd	Ammiel[5a]	6th
		Joah	3rd	Issachar	7th
		Sacar	4th	Peullethai	8th
		Shemaiah's sons: Othni, Rephael, Obed, and Elzabad. Their relatives, Elihu and Semakiah, were capable men. [7]			
	[5b] God had blessed Obed-Edom *with many descendants*. [6] Obed-Edom's son Shemaiah had sons who were leaders in their family, because they were capable men. [8] All these were descendants of Obed-Edom, sixty-two in all. They, their sons, and their relatives were all capable men with strength for the work.				

---

a In the Hebrew text, the phrase "twelve of his sons and relatives" appears after each of the names.
b Also spelled "Asarelah."
c Also spelled "Uzziel."

Merarites[10]	Hosah	Shimri	The chief (who had been appointed so by his father, not being firstborn)
		Hilkiah[11]	2nd
		Tabaliah	3rd
		Zechariah	4th

Gates Assigned by Lot [26:13-19]

[13] They cast lots, young and old, from each family alike, for each gate. [16b] Guard was beside guard.

Gate	Gatekeeper	*Guards* Per Day	Comments
East *Gate*[14]	Shelemiah[a]	6[17]	
North *Gate*	Shelemiah's son Zechariah	4[17]	A wise counselor [14]
South *Gate*[15]	Obed-Edom	4[17]	The storehouses fell to his sons. [15]
West *Gate*[16a]	Shuppim	2[17]	
Shalleketh Gate on the upper road	Hosah	4[17]	

[18] At the courtyard[b] on the west there were four at the road and two at the courtyard *itself.* [19] These were the divisions of the gatekeepers from the descendants of Korah and the descendants of Merari.

Levite Storehouse Officials [26:20-32]

Position	Person(s)	Responsibility
Treasurer[20]	Ahijah[c]	In charge of the storehouses of the temple and the items dedicated *to the* LORD[d]
Assistant	Jehieli [21b] His sons: Zetham and his brother Joel [22a] They were descendants of Ladan, sons of the Gershonites through Ladan, heads of families of Ladan the Gershonite. [21a]	In charge of the treasuries in the temple of the LORD [22b]
The following are Amramites, Izharites, Hebronites, and Uzzielites. [23]		
Assistant[24]	Shubael a descendant of Gershom, son of Moses	Official in charge of the treasuries

---

a   Also spelled "Meshelemiah."
b   Or "the colonnade." The meaning of the Hebrew term *parbar* is not known.
c   From the Masoretic text; Septuagint: "Their fellow Levites."
d   "Items dedicated": objects given to the temple by worshipers.

Assistant [25]	Shelomith and his relatives through Eliezer, *including* Rehabiah, his son Jeshaiah, his son Joram, his son Zicri, and his son Shelomith	[26] In charge of the treasuries *full* of the dedicated things dedicated *for temple use* by King David and the family heads who were commanders of thousands or hundreds, and other army commanders. [27] They dedicated some of the wartime plunder for repairing the temple of the LORD. [28] *They were in charge of* everything that had been dedicated by Samuel the seer, Saul son of Kish, Abner son of Ner, and Joab son of Zeruiah, and all other dedicated things.
Officials [29] and judges over Israel	Kenaniah the Izharite and his descendants	Assigned work outside *the temple*
	Hashabiah the Hebronite and his relatives, 1,700 capable men [30]	Oversight of Israel on the west side of the Jordan for all the work of the LORD and the royal service
	Jeriah [31] the Hebronite chief according to the genealogical records of their families. The records were investigated in the fortieth year of David's reign, and capable men were found among them at Jazer in Gilead. [32] King David appointed him and his 2,700 relatives, who were family heads and capable men, over the Reubenites, the Gadites, and the half-tribe of Manasseh in all the matters *pertaining to* God and *matters pertaining to* the king.	

Army Division Leaders [27:1-15]

[1] This is the registry of the Israelites: the family heads, captains of thousands or hundreds, and their officers who served the king in all matters of the divisions that came into and went out *of active duty* month by month, every month of the year. Each division had 24,000 *men.*

Mo.	Division Leader(s)	Comments
1st	Jashobeam son of Zabdiel, [2a] chief of all commanders, a descendant of Perez [3]	Commanded the first division for the first month. In his division there were 24,000. [2b]
2nd	Dodai the Ahohite, with Mikloth [4]	In his division there were 24,000.
3rd	Benaiah son of Jehoiada the priest [5a]	In his division there were 24,000. [5b] *Also* a mighty warrior among the Thirty. He was over the Thirty. His son Ammizabad was in charge of his division. [6]

4th	Asahel the brother of Joab [7]	His son Zebadiah was his successor and over his division. In his division there were 24,000.
5th	Shamhuth the Izrahite [8]	In his division there were 24,000.
6th	Ira son of Ikkesh the Tekoite [9]	In his division there were 24,000.
7th	Helez the Pelonite [10]	An Ephraimite. In his division there were 24,000.
8th	Sibbecai the Hushathite [11]	A Zerahite. In his division there were 24,000.
9th	Abiezer the Anathothite [12]	A Benjamite. In his division there were 24,000.
10th	Maharai the Netophathite [13]	A Zerahite. In his division there were 24,000.
11th	Benaiah the Pirathonite [14]	An Ephraimite. In his division there were 24,000.
12th	Heldai the Netophathite [15]	From the line of Othniel. In his division there were 24,000.

Israelite Tribal Leaders [27:16-22]	
Tribe	**Leader**
Reuben [16]	Eliezer son of Zicri
Simeon	Shephatiah son of Maacah
Levi [17]	Hashabiah son of Kemuel
Aaron	Zadok was over the descendants of Aaron.[a]
Judah [18]	Elihu, David's brother
Issachar	Omri son of Michael
Zebulun [19]	Ishmaiah son of Obadiah
Naphtali	Jerimoth son of Azriel
Ephraim *half-tribe* [20]	Hoshea son of Azaziah
Manasseh *half*-tribe *east of the Jordan*	Joel son of Pedaiah
Manasseh *half*-tribe in Gilead [21]	Iddo son of Zechariah
Benjamites	Jaasiel son of Abner
Dan [22a]	Azarel son of Jehoram

[22b] These were the leaders of the tribes of Israel. [23] David did not count the Israelites twenty years of age and under, for the Lord had said that he would multiply Israel *until they were* like the stars in the sky. [24] Joab son of Zeruiah had started to count them but did not finish because wrath came upon Israel because of this *census*. The number was not entered in the book History of King David.

---

a   Literally, "was for."

31b All these were the officials in charge of King David's property.

Area	Person	Responsibility Over
Royal storehouses*a* 25	Azmaveth son of Adiel	The royal storehouses
Rural*b* storehouses	Jonathan son of Uzziah	Storehouses in the outlying areas, towns, villages, and watchtowers*c*
Farming 26	Ezri son of Kelub	The workers in the fields tilling the ground
Vineyards 27	Shimei the Ramathite	
Wine storage	Zabdi the Shiphmite	The wine vats*d*
Groves 28	Baal-Hanan the Gederite	The olive and sycamore fig groves in the lowlands
Oil storage	Joash	The stores of olive oil
Herds— in Sharon 29 in the valleys	Shitrai the Sharonite Shaphat son of Adlai	The grazing herds The herds
Camels 30	Obil the Ishmaelite	The camels
Donkeys	Jehdeiah the Meronothite	The donkeys
Flocks 31a	Jaziz the Hagrite	The flocks
Others with Responsibilities		
Counselor	Jonathan, David's uncle 32a Ahithophel 33a	A skillful man, a scribe. And after Ahithophel, then Jehoiada son of Benaiah and Abiathar 34a
Teacher 32b	Jehiel son of Hacmoni	Was with the king's sons
Chief of Staff*e* 33b	Hushai the Arkite	
Royal Army Commander 34b	Joab	

1 Chronicles 28

God Chooses Solomon to Be King and Build the Temple

¹ David assembled all the officials of Israel at Jerusalem: the leaders of tribes, the chief officials of divisions in the service of the king, the commanders of thousands and captains of hundreds *in the army*, the stewards of all the property and livestock of the king and his sons, together with the court officials and the warriors and all the brave, mighty men. ² King David stood on his feet and said,

---

a Or "Treasuries." And next line.
b Or "Regional."
c Or "fortresses."
d Literally, "Over the vineyards for the wine supply."
e Literally, "King's Friend."

"Listen to me, my relatives and my people. I had it in my heart to build a permanent home^a for the ark of the covenant of the Lord, a footstool *for the feet* of our God, so I made preparations to build it. ³ But God said to me, 'You will not build a house for my name, for you are a man of wars and spilled blood.' ⁴ Yet the Lord, the God of Israel, chose me out of all my father's family to be king over Israel forever. He has chosen *the tribe of* Judah as *Israel's* leader, and out of the house of Judah *chosen* my father's house; and out of the sons of my father, he was pleased to make me king over all Israel. ⁵ Out of all my sons (for the Lord has given me many sons), he has chosen my son Solomon to sit on the throne of the kingdom of the Lord over Israel. ⁶ He has said to me, 'Your son Solomon is the one who will build my temple and its courts, for I have chosen him for myself as a son, and I will be a father to him. ⁷ I will establish his kingdom forever if he continues to be steadfast in keeping my commandments and ordinances as he is today.'

⁸ "And now, in the eyes of all Israel, the Lord's assembly, and in the ears of our God, keep and obey^b all the commandments of the Lord your God so that you may possess this good land and bequeath it to your sons after you forever.

⁹ "And you, Solomon my son, know the God of your father and serve him with a whole heart and a willing mind, for the Lord searches all hearts and understands every purpose and thought. If you seek him, he will be found by you; but if you abandon him, he will reject you forever. ¹⁰ Now look, the Lord has chosen you to build a temple for the sanctuary. Be strong and do it."

Plans for the Temple

¹¹ Then David gave to his son Solomon the plans for the temple of the Lord,
including the
porch,
buildings,
storerooms,
upper rooms and inner rooms, and
the place of atonement.^c

¹² And *he gave* the plan for all that was in his mind for the
courts of the temple of the Lord and all the surrounding rooms,
treasuries of silver and gold of the temple of God and
treasuries for the dedicated things,
¹³ the divisions of priests and Levites,
all the work of service in the temple of the Lord, and
all the utensils for service in the Lord's temple: ¹⁴ the
golden *utensils*,
including the weight of gold for *each item for* various kinds of service;

---

a Literally, "a house of rest."
b Literally, "seek out."
c Or "place for the mercy seat."

silver utensils,
>>including the weight of silver for *each item for* various kinds of service;

15 golden lampstands and their golden lamps,
>>*including* the weight of each lampstand and its lamps;

silver lampstands,
>>*including* the weight of each lampstand and its lamps according to the use of each lampstand;

16 table of showbread,
>>*including* the weight of its gold;

silver tables, *including* the weight of its silver; the
>>17 forks, basins, and pitchers of pure gold,
>>>*including* the weight for each;

>>golden bowls,
>>>*including* the weight for each;

>>silver bowls,
>>>*including* the weight for each; and

18 incense altar made of fine gold,
>>*including* the weight; and the

chariot,
>>*meaning* the golden cherubim that spread out *their wings* and covered the ark of the covenant of the LORD.

19 "All *this*," *said David*, "was made clear to me in writing from the hand of the LORD upon me—every detail of this plan." 20 Then David said to his son Solomon, "Be strong and resolute. Do the work. Do not fear or be discouraged, for the LORD God, my God, is with you. He will not fail you or abandon you until all the work for the service of the temple of the LORD is finished. 21 Look, all the divisions of the priests and Levites *are ready* for all the service in the temple of God. Every willing, skilled worker will be with you in all the work for all kinds of service. The leaders and all the people will be completely at your command."

1 Chronicles **29**

David and the People Provide for the Temple

1 Then King David said to the entire assembly, "My son Solomon, the one chosen by God, is young and inexperienced.*a* The work is enormous because the temple is not for man but for the LORD God. 2 I have prepared with all my might for the temple of my God:

the gold for gold *items*
the silver for silver *items*
the bronze for bronze *items*
the iron for iron *items*
the wood for wood *items*

---

a Literally, "tender."

onyx, a pure black stone,^a for the settings

precious stones in all colors

great quantities of marble

³Moreover, in *light of* my delight in the temple of my God, I give to it from my personal wealth—gold and silver—in addition to all I have already provided for this holy temple:

⁴112 tons^b of gold from Ophir^c and

262 tons^d of refined silver to overlay the walls of the buildings.

⁵It is for the gold work and the silver work, all the work to be done by the craftsmen.

Now who *else* is willing today to fill his hand *with gifts* for the LORD?"

⁶The leaders of families, the leaders of the tribes of Israel, the commanders of thousands and of hundreds, and the overseers in charge of the king's work gave willingly. ⁷They gave to the service at the temple of God:

188 tons^e of gold

10,000 gold coins^f

375 tons^g of silver

675 tons^h of bronze

3,750 tonsⁱ of iron

⁸And whoever had precious stones gave them to the treasury of the temple of the LORD in the care of Jehiel the Gershonite. ⁹The people rejoiced because they had offered willingly—because with a whole heart they had given to the LORD willingly. And King David also rejoiced greatly.

David's Prayer Blessing God

¹⁰ So David blessed the LORD in front of all the assembly saying,

"Blessed are you, LORD God of our ancestor Israel, forever and ever. ¹¹ Yours, O LORD, is the greatness, power, glory, splendor, and majesty, for everything in heaven and on earth is yours. Yours is the kingdom, O LORD, and you are lifted up as head over all. ¹² Wealth and honor are from you. You rule over all. Strength and power are in your hand. In your hand is *the ability* to make great and strengthen all. ¹³ Now, we thank you, our God, and praise your glorious name.

¹⁴ "Who am I, and who are my people that we should be able^j to give willingly like this? For everything is from you, and we have given you *only what*

---

a   Literally, "stones of hard, black cement." The exact type of stones referred to in this and the next two lines is uncertain.
b   Literally, "3,000 talents."
c   "Ophir": an unknown place mentioned several times in the Bible as a source of gold and precious stones.
d   Literally, "7,000 talents."
e   Literally, "5,000 talents."
f   Literally, "10,000 darics of gold." "Daric": a coin of ancient Persia.
g   Literally, "10,000 talents."
h   Literally, "18,000 talents."
i   Literally, "100,000 talents."
j   Literally, "should retain strength."

comes from your hand. ¹⁵ We are aliens and nomads before you, like all our ancestors. Our days on earth are like a shadow, without hope. ¹⁶ O Lᴏʀᴅ our God, all this abundance that we have provided to build a temple for your holy name is from your hand—is all owned by you. ¹⁷ I know, my God, that you test hearts, and you are pleased *when people do* what is right. I have given all these things willingly, with a heart *that desires to do* right.ᵃ And now I have seen your people, who are found here, giving to you willingly and joyfully.

¹⁸ O Lᴏʀᴅ, God of our ancestors Abraham, Isaac, and Israel, keep these intentions and desires in the hearts of your people and fix their hearts on you. ¹⁹ Give my son Solomon an undivided heartᵇ to keep your commandments, counsels, and statutes, to do all these things, and to build the temple of God for which I have provided."

Solomon Reaffirmed as King

²⁰ Then David said to all the assembly, "Bless the Lᴏʀᴅ your God!" And the entire assembly blessed the Lᴏʀᴅ, the God of their ancestors, and bowed down, prostrating themselves before the Lᴏʀᴅ and before the king. ²¹ The next day they offered sacrifices to the Lᴏʀᴅ and brought burnt offerings to the Lᴏʀᴅ:

1,000 bulls
1,000 rams
1,000 lambs
drink offerings
great numbers of *other* sacrifices for all Israel

²² They feasted and drank with great joy before the Lᴏʀᴅ that day. They reaffirmed the kingship of Solomon son of David and anointed him before the Lᴏʀᴅ as leader and Zadok as priest. ²³ Solomon sat on the Lᴏʀᴅ's throne as king in his father David's place. He prospered and all Israel obeyed him. ²⁴ All the leaders, the mighty men, and even all King David's sons pledged their allegiance toᶜ King Solomon. ²⁵ The Lᴏʀᴅ made Solomon great and exalted in the eyes of all Israel and bestowed on him royal splendor such as had not been on any king who preceded him in Israel.

²⁶ David son of Jesse ruled over all Israel. ²⁷ The days in which he reigned over Israel totaled forty years. He reigned seven years in Hebron, and he reigned thirty-three in Jerusalem. ²⁸ And so he died at a good old age, satisfied with his days, wealth, and honor. His son Solomon reigned in his place.

²⁹ The acts of King David, from beginning to end, are written among the records of the prophets—the prophet Samuel, the prophet Nathan, and the prophet Gad—³⁰ along with *a description of* his reign and might and the circumstances that came upon him, and upon Israel, and the kingdoms of all the other lands.

---

a   Literally, "with a right heart."
b   Literally, "a whole heart."
c   Literally, "sons gave their hand under."

2 Chronicles

Part 1. Solomon's Reign

God Appears to Solomon

¹ Solomon son of David strengthened himself over his kingdom, and the Lord his God was with him and made him exceedingly great. ² Solomon spoke to all Israel: to the commanders of thousands and hundreds *in the army*, to the judges, and to all the leading men in Israel, the heads of families. ³ Solomon went to the high place at Gibeon with all the assembly with him, because God's meeting tent, which Moses the servant of the Lord had made in the wilderness, was there. ⁴ Now David had brought the ark of God up from Kiriath Jearim to Jerusalem, for he had pitched a tent for it and prepared a place for it there. ⁵ He put the bronze altar made by Bezalel son of Uri, son of Hur,ᵃ in front of the tabernacle of the Lord. And Solomon and the assembly sought God there. ⁶ Solomon went up there before the Lord to the bronze altar, which was at the meeting tent, and offered one thousand burnt offerings on it. ⁷ That night God appeared to Solomon *in a dream* and said, "Ask me—what shall I give you?"

⁸ Solomon said to God, "You showed great lovingkindness to David, and you have made me king in his place. ⁹ Now, Lord God, confirm your word with my father David, for you have made me king over a people as numerous as the dust on the earth. ¹⁰ Now, give me wisdom and understanding to lead this people,ᵇ for who can govern this great people of yours?"

¹¹ God answered Solomon,

"Because
this is in your heart,ᶜ and because
you did not ask for riches, wealth, honor, or the deathᵈ of your enemies, or
even long life, but
you have asked for wisdom and understanding,
that you may govern my people over whom I have made you king,
¹² wisdom and understanding are given to you.
I am also giving you wealth, riches, and honor
such as no king before you has had and aboveᵉ what any king after you shall
have."

¹³ Then Solomon went from the high place at Gibeon, from before the meeting tent, to Jerusalem, and he reigned over Israel. ¹⁴ Solomon acquired chariots

---

a See Exodus 27:1–8.
b Literally, "to go out before this people and come in."
c Literally, "Because it is thus with your heart."
d Literally, "the life."
e Literally, "not like."

and horses; he had 1,400 chariots and 12,000 horsemen, whom he kept in chariot cities and also with himself in Jerusalem. ¹⁵ The king made gold and silver in Jerusalem *as common* as stones and cedar *as abundant* as sycamore fig trees in the foothills. ¹⁶ Solomon imported his horses from Egypt and Kue.ᵃ The royal merchants bought them from Kue at market value.ᵇ ¹⁷ A chariot was imported from Egypt for fourteen poundsᶜ of silver and a horse for three and a half pounds.ᵈ And they would export them by the hand *of their agents* to all the kings of the Hittites and the Arameans.

Labor and Materials for the Temple

¹ Solomon gave the order to begin to build the temple for the name of the Lᴏʀᴅ and a palace for himself. ² He assignedᵉ 70,000 *men* as porters, 80,000 as stonecutters in the hills, and 3,600 as foremen over them.

³ He sent *envoys* to Hiram king of Tyre, saying,

"*Do for me as* you did for my father David when you sent him cedar *logs* to build his palace. ⁴ Look, I am about to build a temple for the name of the Lᴏʀᴅ my God and dedicate it to him—for burning sweet incense and setting out showbread before him continually, for burnt offerings morning and evening, and for Sabbaths, New Moon *Festivals*, and appointed festivals of the Lᴏʀᴅ our God. This is *meant to be* for Israel forever.

⁵ "The temple that I am building will be great, for our God is greater than all gods. ⁶ Who is ableᶠ to build temple for him, for the heavens, even the highest heavens, cannot bear his glory!ᵍ So who am I, that I should build a temple for him, except *as a place* to burn incense before him? ⁷ Now

send me a man

skilled at working with gold and silver, bronze and iron, and purple, crimson, and blue *fabrics*; and

skilled at engraving,

to be with the other craftsmen who are *here* with me in Judah and Jerusalem, whom my father David provided.

⁸ Send me cedar, juniper, and algum logs from Lebanon,

for I know that your servants know how to cut timber in Lebanon.

Look, my workers will be with your workers

⁹ to prepare many logs for me,

because the temple I am building will be great and awe-inspiring.

---

a "Kue": a.k.a. Tarsus, the chief city of Cilicia.
b Literally, "for a price."
c Literally, "600 *shekels.*"
d Literally, "150 *shekels.*"
e Literally, "He counted."
f Literally, "Who retains power."
g From the Septuagint; Masoretic text: "cannot contain him."

¹⁰ Look, I will give your servants the woodsmen who cut the timber,
130,000 bushels of crushed wheat,
130,000 bushels of barley,
120,000 gallons of wine, and
120,000 gallons of olive oil."^a

¹¹ Hiram king of Tyre replied to Solomon in a letter, which he sent to him:

> ### Hiram
> ### King of Persia
>
> To Solomon:
> Because the LORD loves his people, he has made you king over them. ¹² Blessed^b be the LORD, the God of Israel, who made the heavens and the earth! He has given King David a wise son who knows discretion and prudence, who will build a temple for the LORD and a palace for his kingdom. ¹³ Now I have sent you Huram-Abi, a skilled man with insight and understanding. ¹⁴ He is the son of a woman from the daughters of Dan, and his father is a man of Tyre. He knows how to work with gold, silver, bronze, iron, stone, and wood, and with purple *and* blue fine linen and crimson *fabric*, as well as to make any kind of engraving and execute any plan that may be given to him. He will be with your skilled men and those of my lord, your father David. ¹⁵ Now may my lord send to his servants the wheat, barley, oil, and wine of which he has spoken. ¹⁶ We will cut all the timber from Lebanon that you need and bring them on rafts by sea to Joppa, so you can take them up to Jerusalem.

¹⁷ Then Solomon took a census of all the foreigners in the land of Israel after the census his father David had taken. There were found to be 153,600. ¹⁸ He made 70,000 of them porters, 80,000 of them stonecutters in the mountains, and 3,600 of them foremen to keep the people working.

3 *2 Chronicles*

Building the Temple

¹ Solomon began to build the temple of the LORD in Jerusalem on Mount Moriah, where *the Lord* had appeared to his father David *to tell him* that he should prepare a place at the threshing floor of Araunah^c the Jebusite. ² He began to build in late April^d of the fourth year of his reign.

---

a Literally, respectively, "20,000 cors" twice, "20,000 baths" twice.
b In the Hebrew text, this is preceded by "Hiram also said."
c Literally, "Ornan": an alternate spelling of Araunah.
d Literally, "on the second day of the second month."

Temple Specifications [3:3-4:16]

³ He made these:

Foundation These are *the measurements*[a] *of* the foundations for the temple of God. ³

Length	90 ft. ³
Width	30 ft.[b] ³

Front Porch

Location	In front of the main hall ⁴
Width	30 ft.,[c] the same width as the temple ⁴
Height	30 ft. ⁴
Inside Overlay	Pure gold ⁴

House

Decoration	Precious stones and gold from Parvaim[d] ⁶
	Engraved cherubim on the walls ⁷
	Gold overlay on the rafters, doorposts, walls, and doors ⁷
Main Room	
Material	Juniper logs overlaid with fine gold ⁵
Decoration	Palm trees and ornamental chains over the logs ⁵
Upper Rooms	
Decoration	Gold overlay ⁹
Most Holy Place	
Length	30 ft. ⁸
Width	30 ft. ⁸
Nails	*Each made of* 20 ounces[e] of gold ⁹
Overlay	22½ tons[f] of gold ⁸
Cherubim	
Type	Sculptured ¹⁰
Number	2 ¹⁰
Overlay	Gold ¹⁰
Wingspan	Together, 30 ft. ¹¹⁻¹³
	Each outside wing: 7½ ft long and touching the wall
	Each inside wing: 7½ ft.[g] long, attached at the wingtips
Position	On their feet facing the main room ¹³
Dividing Curtain	
Material	Blue, purple, and crimson *wool* and fine white linen ¹⁴
Design	Cherubim woven into it ¹⁴

a All lengths are in cubits in the manuscripts. A cubit is approximately 18 inches.
b Literally, "60 cubits" and "20 cubits," respectively, "using the old standard of cubit."
c Literally "20 cubits." And next line and twice in verse 8.
d "Parvaim": an unknown place.
e Literally, "50 shekels."
f Literally, "600 talents."
g Literally, "20 cubits" and "5 cubits" twice.

Pillars

Number	2 [15]
Location	Front of the temple [15, 17]
	One to the right, named Jakin; and one to the left, named Boaz [17]
Height	52½ ft. [15]
Top Decoration	7½ ft. tall[a] [15] bowl-shaped [4:12]
	Ornamental chains made as in the inner sanctuary with 100 pomegranates, attached to the capitals [3:16]

4 *2 Chronicles*

Bronze Altar

Length	30 ft. [1]
Width	30 ft. [1]
Height	15 ft.[c] [1]

Sea	*A large washbasin*
Purpose	For the priests to wash in [6]
Location	The southeast corner [10]
Material	Cast *bronze* [2]
Shape	Round
Circumference	45 ft. [2]
Diameter[b]	15 ft. [2]
Height	7½ ft.[d] [2]
Decoration	Oxen encircling it beneath the brim, each 2 in. long,[e] surrounding the sea in 2 rows, cast in one piece with the rest [3]
Base Design	12 oxen, 3 facing each direction (north, east, south, and west), with their hindquarters facing the center, the Sea on top of them [4]
Bowl	
Thickness	3 in.[f] [5]
Brim	*Shaped* like the brim of a cup, like a lily blossom [5]
Capacity	18,000 gallons[g] [5]
Location	Right, southeast corner [10]

---

a Literally, "35 cubits" and "5 cubits."
b Literally, "Brim to Brim."
c Literally, "20 cubits" twice and "10 cubits."
d Literally, "30 cubits," "10 cubits," and "5 cubits."
e Literally, "10 per cubit."
f Literally, "a handbreadth."
g Literally, "3,000 baths." The capacity is difficult to reconcile geometrically and mathematically, perhaps due to lost understanding of ancient measurements.

Basins	
Purpose	To rinse items *used in making* the burnt offerings [6]
Number	10 [6]
Location	5 on the south side and 5 on the north side[a] [6]
Lampstands	
Design	As prescribed [7]
Material	Gold [7]
Number	10 [7]
Location	In the temple: 5 on the south side and 5 on the north side [7]
Tables	
Number	10 [8]
Location	In the temple: 5 on the south side and 5 on the north side [8]
Finger Bowls	
Number	100
Material	Gold
Utensils	
Type	Pots, shovels, forks [16]
Material	Polished bronze [16]

[9] Then he made the court of the priests and the great courtyard with its doors, and he overlaid their doors with bronze. [10] And he placed the Sea on the right side at the southeast corner. [11] Huram also made the pots, shovels, and bowls.

So Huram finished doing the work for King Solomon in the temple of the LORD:
[12] two pillars
   two bowl-shaped capitals[b] on top of the pillars
   two netlike works covering the bowl-shaped capitals on top of the pillars
[13] four hundred pomegranates for the two netlike works that decorated the two bowl-shaped capitals on top of the pillars,
      two rows of pomegranates per net
[14] stands with their basins
[15] Sea with the twelve oxen under it
[16] Pots, shovels, and *fire* forks, and all the equipment for these were made by Huram-Abi of burnished bronze for the temple of the LORD.
   [17] The king had them cast in clay molds in the Jordan plain between Succoth and Zarethan. [18] Solomon made all the utensils in great quantities, such that the weight of the bronze was not determined.
[19] Solomon also made the furnishings that were in the temple of God:
   golden altar
   tables for the bread of the Presence
   [20] lampstands with their lamps of pure gold
      that burned in front of the inner sanctuary in the way prescribed

---

a   Literally, "5 to the right and 5 to the left." And verses 7–8.
b   "Capitals": the decorative topmost part of a pillar.

²¹ flowers
lamps
tongs of gold (the purest gold)
²² snuffers
bowls
spoons
firepans ⎬ of pure gold

entrance to the temple
inner doors for the Most Holy Place
doors of the temple's main hall ⎬ of gold

5 2 Chronicles

The Lord Enters the Temple

¹ So all the work that King Solomon did for the temple of the LORD was finished. Then Solomon brought in all the articles David his father had dedicated. He stored the silver, the gold, and all the utensils in the treasury of the temple of God.

² Then Solomon assembled in Jerusalem the elders of Israel, all the heads of the tribes, and the heads of families in Israel, to bring up the ark of the covenant of the LORD from the City of David, which is Zion. ³ In early autumn,[a] all the Israelite men assembled to the king at the Festival *of Shelters.* ⁴ All the elders of Israel came, and the Levites took up the ark. ⁵ The Levitical priests brought up the ark, the meeting tent, and all the holy articles in the tent.

⁶ King Solomon and the whole congregation of Israel that had gathered around him were with him before the ark. They were sacrificing so many sheep and cattle that they could not be counted or recorded. ⁷ The priests brought the ark of the covenant of the LORD to its place, the inner sanctuary of the temple, the Most Holy Place, beneath the wings of the cherubim. ⁸ The cherubim spread their wings over the place of the ark, such that they covered the ark and its *carrying* poles from above. ⁹ The poles were so long that their ends were visible in the front of the inner sanctuary (*i.e., the Holy Place*), but they were not visible from outside. They are there to this day. ¹⁰ There was nothing in the ark except the two tablets that Moses put there at Mount Horeb, where the LORD made[b] *the covenant* with the Israelites after they came out of Egypt.

¹¹ When the priests went out from the Holy Place
(for all the priests who were present had sanctified themselves regardless of their divisions),
¹² all the Levitical musicians of Asaph, Heman, Jeduthun, and their sons and kinsmen
were clothed in fine linen
and playing cymbals, harps, and lyres—
standing on the east side of the altar,
and 120 priests were with them sounding trumpets.

---

a Literally, "the seventh month."
b Literally, "cut."

¹³ The trumpeters and musicians sounded as one to praise and thank the Lord. When

> they lifted up their voice,
>> accompanied by trumpets, cymbals, and other musical instruments, and they praised the Lord,
>>> *saying,* "He is good; his lovingkindness endures forever,"

then

> the temple, the house of the Lord, was filled with a cloud.
>> ¹⁴ The priests were not able to stand and minister because of the cloud, for the glory of the Lord filled the temple of God.

2 Chronicles **6**

Solomon Addresses Israel

¹ Then Solomon said, "The Lord said he would dwell in thick darkness. ² I have built a magnificent temple for you, a place for you to dwell forever." ³ Then the king turned his face to the whole congregation of Israel and blessed them while they were standing: ⁴ He said,

"Blessed be the Lord, the God of Israel, who spoke by his mouth to my father David and fulfilled it with his hand, saying,

> ⁵ 'From the day when I brought my people out of Egypt, I have not chosen a city out of all the tribes of Israel to build a temple to bear my name.^a Neither did I choose a man to be leader over my people Israel. ⁶ But *now* I have chosen Jerusalem for my name to be there, and I have chosen David to be over my people Israel.'

⁷ "It was in my father David's heart to build a temple for the name of the Lord, the God of Israel. ⁸ But the Lord said to my father David,

> 'Since it was in your heart to build a temple for my name (and you did well that it was in your heart), ⁹ nevertheless, you shall not build the temple. Rather, your son, who will come from your own body, he will build the temple for my name.'

¹⁰ "The Lord has fulfilled the word he spoke, and I have risen in my father David's place. I sit on the throne of Israel, just as the Lord said, and I have built the temple for the name of the Lord, the God of Israel. ¹¹ And that is where I have put the ark containing the covenant of the Lord, which he made with the people of^b Israel."

Solomon's Dedication Prayer

¹² Then Solomon stood before the altar of the Lord in front of the entire congregation of Israel and spread out his hands. ¹³ Solomon had made a bronze platform and placed it in the middle of the courtyard. It was seven and a half feet long, seven and a half feet wide, and four and a half feet high.^c He stood on it, knelt on his knees before the whole assembly of Israel, spread out his hands to heaven, ¹⁴ and said,

---

a Literally, "for my name to be there."
b Literally, "sons of."
c Literally, "5, 5, 3 cubits," respectively.

Preamble

"O Lᴏʀᴅ, God of Israel,

there is no God on heaven or earth who is like you, who keeps a covenant of loyal love with your servants who walk before you wholeheartedly.

¹⁵ You kept what you promised to your servant David, my father. You spoke it with your mouth and have fulfilled it with your hand today.

¹⁶ Now therefore, Lᴏʀᴅ God of Israel,

carry out for your servant David my father that which you promised him, saying,

'You shall not lack a man*a* to sit before me on the throne of Israel, provided your descendants guard their ways and walk in my Law, just as you have walked before me.'

¹⁷ And now, Lᴏʀᴅ God of Israel,

let the promise that you spoke to your servant David come true.

¹⁸ But will God really dwell on earth with humans?

Look, the heavens, even the highest heavens, cannot contain you! How much less can this temple I have built!

¹⁹ Turn toward your servant's prayer and his supplication, O Lᴏʀᴅ my God,

to hear his cry and his prayer that your servant has prayed before you.

²⁰ Open your eyes toward this temple day and night,

toward the place where you promised to put your name,

to hear the prayers that your servant will pray toward this place.

²¹ Hear the prayers of your servant and your people when they pray toward this place.

Hear from your dwelling place in heaven. Listen and forgive!

Requests

²² "If anyone sins against their neighbor and is obliged to take an oath, and comes to take an oath before your altar in this temple,

²³ may you hear from heaven and act and judge your servants,

repaying the guilty by bringing their ways upon their own heads and vindicating the righteous by rewarding them according to their righteousness.

²⁴ If your people Israel are defeated by the enemy because they have sinned against you, but then repent, confess your name, pray, and plead before you in this temple,

²⁵ then may you hear from heaven and forgive your people Israel's sins.

May you return them to the land that you gave to them and their ancestors.

²⁶ "When the skies are shut up and there is no rain because they have sinned against you, but then they pray to this place, confess your name, and turn from their sin because you have afflicted them,

---

a Literally, "not have cut off a man."

²⁷ then may you hear from heaven and forgive the sins of your servants, your people Israel.

May you teach them the good way in which they should walk.

May you send rain upon the land that you have given to your people as an inheritance.

²⁸ If there is

famine in the land,

plague,

blight or mildew,

locust or grasshopper, or

if enemies besiege them in the land of any of their cities, or

if there be any plague or any sickness,

²⁹ then

if there is any prayer or any supplication from any person or by all your people Israel—each knowing their own suffering and their own grief, spreading out their hands toward this temple—

³⁰ then may you

hear from heaven, your dwelling place, and

forgive and

give to each person according to all their ways,

since you know the heart. You alone know the human heart[a]—

³¹ so that they may fear you and walk in your ways all the days they live on the face of the earth. ³² And also,

when a foreigner who is not from your people Israel

comes from a distant land

on account of your great reputation,[b] strong hand, and outstretched arm, and they

come and pray toward this temple,

³³ then may you

hear from heaven, your dwelling place, and

do everything that the foreigner cries out for you *to do*

so that all the peoples of the earth may

know your name and

fear you, just as your people Israel do, and

know that this temple I have built is called by your name.

³⁴ "When your people

go out to fight against their enemies, wherever you send them, and

pray to you toward this city that you have chosen and the temple I have built for your name,

³⁵ then

may you hear their prayer and supplication from heaven.

May you do justice on their behalf.

---

a Literally, "the hearts of the sons of men."
b Literally, "great name."

³⁶ "If

> they sin against you (for there is no one who never sins), and
> you are angry with them, and
> you deliver them to their enemy,
>> who takes them captive to a land far or near;

³⁷ but they

> turn their hearts back *to you* in the land where they were taken as captives and
> turn and beseech your favor in the land of their captors,
>> confessing, 'We have sinned, committed iniquity, and acted wickedly';
>> ³⁸ and they
> turn to you with all their hearts and souls in the land of their captors where
> they were taken as captives, and they
> pray
>> toward their land that you gave to their ancestors,
>> *toward* the city that you chose,
>> toward the temple that I have built for your name;

³⁹ then may you

> hear their prayer and supplication from heaven, your dwelling place,
> do *justice* on their behalf, and
> forgive your people, who have sinned against you.

⁴⁰ "Now, my God,

> I pray that your eyes will be open and your ears attentive to a prayer
> offered in this place.

⁴¹ O Lᴏʀᴅ God,

> rise up;
> come into your resting place, you and the ark of your might.
> Let your priests, O Lᴏʀᴅ God, be clothed with righteousness, and
> let your godly ones rejoice in your goodness.

⁴² O Lᴏʀᴅ God,

> do not turn away from the face of your anointed;
> remember your loyal love for your servant David."

7 2 Chronicles

Dedication Sacrifices

¹ When Solomon finished praying, fire came down from heaven and consumed the burnt offering and the sacrifices, and the glory of the Lᴏʀᴅ filled the temple of the Lᴏʀᴅ. ² And the priests were not able to enter the temple of the Lᴏʀᴅ, because the glory of the Lᴏʀᴅ filled the temple of the Lᴏʀᴅ. ³ When all the Israelites saw the fire come down and the glory of the Lᴏʀᴅ over the temple, they bowed down with their faces to the ground on the pavement and worshiped and praised the Lᴏʀᴅ, *saying,* "He is good; his loyal love endures forever."

⁴ Then the king and all the people offered sacrifices before the Lᴏʀᴅ. ⁵ King Solomon offered a sacrifice of 22,000 oxen and 120,000 sheep and goats. Thus the

king and all the people dedicated the temple of God. [6] The priests took their positions, as did the Levites, with instruments for music to the Lord, which King David had made for praising the Lord, saying, "For his loyal love endures forever"—whenever David gave praise using them.[a] The priests were blowing trumpets opposite them, and all the Israelites were standing. [7] Solomon consecrated the middle of the courtyard in front of the temple of the Lord, for he sacrificed burnt offerings and the fat of fellowship offerings there, because the bronze altar that Solomon had made was not able to hold the burnt offerings, grain offerings, and fat portions.

[8] Solomon gave a seven-day feast during that time, and all the Israelites—an exceedingly great assembly, *with people* from Lebo Hamath *up north* all the way *down* to the Wadi Egypt—were *celebrating* with him. [9] On the eighth day they held a solemn assembly, for they had observed the dedication of the temple for seven days and the Festival *of Shelters* for seven *more* days. [10] On the twenty-third day of the seventh month,[b] Solomon sent the people away to their homes rejoicing and in good spirits because of all the good things the Lord had done for David, for Solomon, and for his people Israel.

[11] So Solomon successfully finished the temple of the Lord, the king's palace, and all that entered his heart to do for the temple of the Lord and his own palace.

God's Response

[12] Then the Lord appeared to Solomon at night and said to him,
"I have heard your prayer and chosen this place for myself to be a house of sacrifice.

[13] "If I shut up the sky so that there is no rain, or
if I command the locust to devour *all vegetation on the* land, or
if I send a plague on my people,
[14] then
if my people, who are called by my name, will
humble themselves,
pray,
seek my face, and
turn from their wicked ways,
then I will
hear from heaven,
forgive their sins, and
heal their land.

[15] "Now my eyes will be open and my ears attentive to the prayers *offered in* this place.
[16] For I have consecrated this temple for my name to be there forever.
My eyes and my heart will always be there. [17] As for you,
if you
walk before me just as your father David walked, and
do all that I command you,
keeping my statutes and judgments,

---

a Literally, "in David's praising by their hand."
b About October 1.

¹⁸ then I will establish your royal throne
>> as I covenanted with your father David,
>>> saying, 'You will not lack a ruler*^a* for Israel.'
¹⁹ But if you
>> turn away and abandon my statutes and commandments that I put before you, and
>> walk after and serve other gods, bowing down to them,
²⁰ then I will
>> uproot Israel from the land I gave them,
>> thrust from before my face this temple that I consecrated to my name, and
>> make *Israel* a proverb and taunt among all the peoples.
>>> ²¹ This temple is eminent *today—but then* all who pass by it will be appalled and say,
>>>> 'Why did the Lord do this to this land and this temple?'
>>> ²² They'll answer, 'Because
>>>> they abandoned the Lord,
>>>>> the God of their ancestors, who brought them up out of Egypt, and they embraced other gods—
>>>>> bowed down to them and served them.
>>>> Therefore he has brought all this disaster upon them.' "

8 2 Chronicles

Temple Construction Completed

¹ After twenty years, in which Solomon had built the temple and his own palace,
>> ² he rebuilt the cities that Hiram had given him and settled Israelites in them.
>> ³ Then Solomon went to Hamath-Zobah and captured it.
>> ⁴ He built
>>> Tadmor in the desert and
>>> all the store cities that he built in Hamath. ⁵ He built
>>> Upper Beth Horon and Lower Beth Horon, fortified cities—
>>>> with walls and gates with bars— ⁶ and also
>>> Baalath and
>>> all the store cities that he had, and
>>> all the cities for chariots and the cities for cavalry.
>> Solomon built everything that pleased him in Jerusalem, Lebanon, and all the land under his rule.

^{8b} Solomon conscripted as slave labor
>>> ⁷ all the remaining people from the Amorites, Hittites, Perizzites, Hivites, and Jebusites, who were not Israelites, ^{8a} but were
>>>> descendants of those *pagans* who remained in the land,
>>>> those whom the Israelites had not killed, ^{8c} as it is to this day. ⁹ But
>> Solomon did not make slaves out of the Israelites for his work. They became soldiers, high officers, chariot officers, and cavalrymen. ¹⁰ These were the chief officials of King Solomon: 250 who ruled over the people.

---

a   Literally, "not have cut off a man."

[11] Solomon brought Pharaoh's daughter up from the City of David to the house that he had built for her,

> for he said, "My wife shall not live in the house of David king of Israel,
>> for the places where the ark of the Lord has entered are holy." [12] Then

Solomon offered burnt offerings to the Lord
> on the altar of the Lord, which he'd built in front of the *temple* porch.
>> [13] He followed the daily requirement for offerings according to the command of Moses for Sabbaths, New Moon *Festivals,* and the three annual festivals: the Festival of Unleavened Bread, the Festival of Weeks, and the Festival of Shelters.

[14] He appointed
> the divisions of priests for their service,
> the Levites for their duties to *lead* praise and to serve along with the priests
>> according to the regulation of his father David and the daily requirement,
> the gatekeepers in their divisions at every gate;
>> for this was the command of David the man of God. [15] And they did not deviate from the king's command to the priests and Levites in any matter or concerning the storehouses.[a]

[16] So all Solomon's work was carried out from the day the foundation of the temple of the Lord was laid until it was finished. So the temple of the Lord was completed. [17] Then Solomon went to Ezion-Geber and Eilat on the seacoast of Edom. [18] And Hiram sent him ships manned by his servants, ships and servants who knew the sea. They went to Ophir[b] together with Solomon's servants, and they took seventeen tons[c] of gold from there and brought it to King Solomon.

2 Chronicles 9

The Queen of Sheba Visits

[1] Now when the Queen of Sheba[d] heard about Solomon's fame, she *came* to Jerusalem to test him with difficult questions. She had a tremendous entourage—camels bearing spices and great quantities of gold and precious stones. She came to Solomon and spoke to him about everything that was on her mind. [2] Solomon explained every matter to her. Nothing was too obscure for Solomon to explain.
[3] When the Queen of Sheba saw

> Solomon's wisdom,
> the palace he had built,
> [4] the food on his table,

> the seating of his officials,
> his attending ministers and their attire,
> his cupbearers[e] and their attire, and
> the burnt offerings that he offered in the temple of the Lord,[f]

she was breathless *with amazement.*

---

a Or "the treasuries."
b "Ophir": an unknown place mentioned several times in the Bible as a source of gold and precious stones.
c Literally, "450 talents."
d "Sheba": a place whose location is unknown. Popular theories identify it with Ethiopia or Yemen.
e "Cupbearers": a king's closest and most trusted servants.
f From the Septuagint; Masoretic text: "and the steps by which he went up to the temple of the Lord."

[5] She said to the king, "The report I heard in my own country about your affairs and your wisdom was true, [6] but I did not believe their words until I came and saw it with my own eyes. Look, I was not told of half the abundance of your wisdom! You have surpassed the report I heard. [7] How blessed are your men, and how blessed are these servants who stand before you continually and listen to your wisdom! [8] Blessed be the LORD your God, who delighted in you and put you on his throne as king for the LORD your God. Because your God loved Israel and would establish them forever, he has placed you over them to do justice and righteousness."

[9] Then she gave the king four and a half tons[a] of gold and a huge quantity of spices and precious stones. There has never been anything like the spices the Queen of Sheba gave to King Solomon.

> [10] (In addition, the servants of Hiram and the servants of Solomon, who brought gold from Ophir, *also* brought algum wood[b] and precious stones. [11] From the algum wood, the king made steps for the temple of the LORD and for the king's palace, and lyres and harps for the singers. Nothing like them had been seen before in the land of Judah.)

[12] So King Solomon gave the Queen of Sheba all she desired, whatever she asked for, *more than* what she had brought to him. Then she turned and went to her own country (*i.e.*, she and her servants).

Solomon's Wealth 9:1-28

All the kings of the Arabs and governors of the country brought gold and silver to Solomon. [14b] Others brought gifts of silver and gold articles, garments, weapons, spices, horses, and mules, so much[a] year after year. [24]

Income	
Tribute	25 tons[b] of Gold were brought to Solomon each year. [13] Plus
Taxes & gifts	*that* brought in by merchants and traveling traders. [14a]
Decorative Shields	The king put them in the Palace of the Forest of Lebanon. [16b]
Large Shields	200 made with 15 lb. of hammered gold [15]
Small Shields	300 made with 7½ lb.[c] of hammered gold [16a]
Great Throne	The king made the great throne. [17]
Material	Ivory [17]
Overlay	Fine gold [17]
Steps	Six [18]
Footstool	Of gold, attached to it [18]
Armrests	On each side[d] of the seat [18]
Lion *Statues*	Two, standing beside the armrests [18]
	Twelve stood there, on the six steps, *one* on each side [19]

Nothing like it had been made for any other kingdom. [19]

---

a Literally, "120 talents."
b "Algum wood": Its identity is uncertain.
a Or "so," meaning at a set rate (perhaps referring to tribute from conquered people).
b Literally, "666 talents."
c Literally, "600 *shekels*" and "300 *shekels*," respectively.
d Literally, "On this *side and* on that *side.*"

Drinking Vessels	
Material	
King Solomon's	Gold [20a]
All other vessels	Gold [20a]

Silver was not considered valuable in the days of Solomon. [20b] He made silver as *common* as stones in Jerusalem and cedars *as abundant* as sycamore fig trees in the foothills. [27]

Trading Ships	The king's ships went to trade,[a] manned by the servants of Hiram. Once every three years trading ships would come *back* loaded with gold, silver, ivory, apes, and baboons. [21]

Military Forces	
Horsemen	12,000, stationed in the chariot cities and with the king in Jerusalem
Stalls	4,000 [25]

Solomon's horses were imported from Egypt and from every land. [28]

Summary
[22] King Solomon grew greater than all the kings of the earth in wealth and wisdom. [23] All the kings of the world were seeking Solomon's face to hear the wisdom God had put in his heart.

9:24 follows 9:14 above

[26] He ruled over all the kings from the *Euphrates* River to the land of the Philistines, all the way to the border of Egypt.

The Death of Solomon

[29] The rest of the acts of Solomon, from beginning to end, are recorded in the book of Nathan the prophet, in the prophecy of Ahijah the Shilonite, and in the *scroll* Visions of Iddo the Seer (concerning Jeroboam son of Nebat). [30] For forty years Solomon reigned over all Israel in Jerusalem. [31] Then Solomon lay down with his ancestors, and they buried him in the city of his father David. His son Rehoboam reigned in his place.

Part 2. The Divided Kingdom

2 Chronicles 10

Rehoboam Loses Control of Israel

[1] Rehoboam went to Shechem, for all Israel had gone to Shechem to crown him king. [2] When Jeroboam son of Nebat heard about this, he returned from Egypt. (He was in Egypt because he had fled from King Solomon.[b]) [3] The leaders of *Northern* Israel sent[c] messengers to summon him. Jeroboam and all Israel came and contended with Rehoboam. [4] They said, "Your father made our yoke difficult. Now lighten the hard labor of your father and the heavy yoke he put on us, and we will serve you."

[5] *The king* told them, "Return to me in three days." So the people went away.

---

a Literally, "to Tarshish with." The city's name became a metaphor for "trade."
b See 1 Kings 11:40.
c Literally, "They sent."

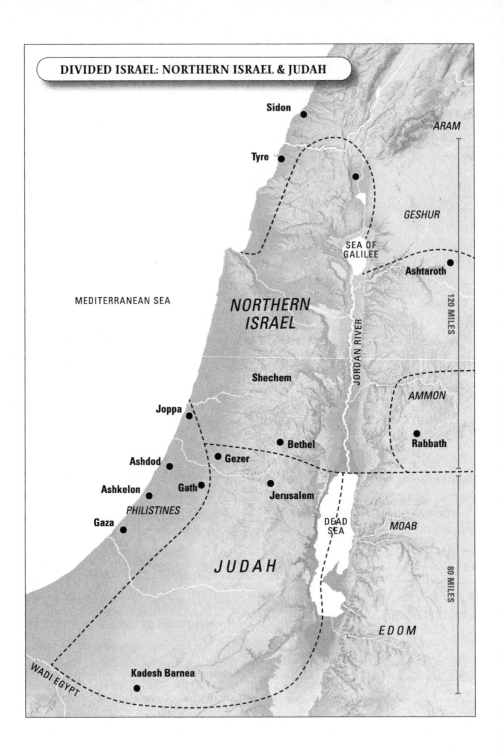

DIVIDED ISRAEL: NORTHERN ISRAEL & JUDAH

Sidon

ARAM

Tyre

GESHUR

SEA OF
GALILEE

Ashtaroth

MEDITERRANEAN SEA

NORTHERN
ISRAEL

120 MILES

JORDAN RIVER

Shechem

AMMON

Joppa

Bethel

Rabbath

Ashdod

Gezer

Ashkelon

Gath

Jerusalem

PHILISTINES

Gaza

DEAD
SEA

MOAB

80 MILES

JUDAH

EDOM

WADI EGYPT

Kadesh Barnea

⁶ King Rehoboam conferred with the elders who had served*a* Solomon when he was alive, saying, "How do you advise me to answer these people?"

⁷ They advised him, "If you will be good to these people, appease them—speak good words to them—then they will be your servants for life."

⁸ But he ignored the counsel the elders gave him and conferred with the young men who grew up with him and served him. ⁹ He asked them, "How do you advise me to answer these people who have said to me, 'Lighten the yoke your father put on us'?"

¹⁰ The young men who grew up with him answered, "Tell this to the people who said to you, 'Your father made our yoke heavy, now lighten it for us.' Tell them: 'My little finger is thicker than my father's waist. ¹¹ Now my father did put a heavy yoke on you, and I'll add to it. My father scourged you with whips, but I will scourge you with scorpions.'"

¹² Jeroboam and all the people came to Rehoboam on the third day, just as the king had directed, "Return to me on the third day." ¹³ The king answered them harshly and ignored the counsel of the elders. ¹⁴ He spoke to them guided by the advice of the young men, saying, "My father made your yoke heavy, and I'll add to it. My father scourged you with whips, but I will scourge you with scorpions!"

¹⁵ The king did not listen to the people, for this was a turn of events from God so that the Lᴏʀᴅ might fulfill the word he spoke through Ahijah the Shilonite to Jeroboam son of Nebat.*b*

¹⁶ When all the Israelites *saw* that the king had not listened to them, they replied to the king,

"What do we care about*c* David?

We have no interest*d* in Jesse's son.

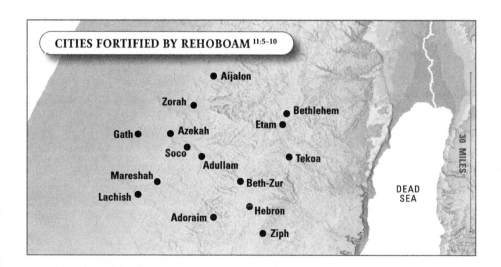

CITIES FORTIFIED BY REHOBOAM ¹¹:⁵⁻¹⁰

---

a Literally, "had stood before." And verse 8.
b See 1 Kings 11:29-39.
c Literally, "What portion do we have in."
d Literally, "no inheritance."

Timeline of Kings and Prophets

GOOD	GOOD turned BAD
BAD	BAD turned GOOD

Years BC

Prophets are in italics. Their location on the table does not indicate the kingdom of their ministry. Since the time of the ministry of some of the prophets is uncertain, a question mark follows their name, and they appear two or three times.

Years BC	Judah Prophets	Judah	United/Northern Kings	Northern Kingdom	Prophets
1079	*Samuel*				
1007			SAUL		
			DAVID		*Nathan* *Gad*
970		**Judah**	SOLOMON	**Northern Kingdom**	
931	*Iddo*				
915	*Shemaiah*	REHOBOAM		JEROBOAM 1	*Ahijah*
912		ABIJAH			
	Azariah			NADAB	
				BAASHA	
	Jehu	ASA		ELAH	
				ZIMRI	
				OMRI	
971	*Hanani*			AHAB	*Elijah* *Micaiah*
	Obadiah?			AHAZIAH	
	Eliezer Joel?	JEHOSHAPHAT	JEHORAM	JORAM	
849					
842	*Obadiah?*		AHAZIAH		
841		ATHALIAH (QUEEN)		JEHU	*Elisha*
836					
		JOASH		JEHOAHAZ	
797					
		AMAZIAH		JEHOASH	
768				JEROBOAM II	*Jonah?*
		UZZIAH		ZECHARIAH	*Amos*
				SHALLUM	
751	*Isaiah*			MENAHEM	
		JOTHAM		PEKAHIAH	*Hosea*
732	*Micah*			PEKAH	
	Oded	AHAZ		HOSHEA	
716					
687		HEZEKIAH			
		MANASSEH			
643		AMON	*Nahum*		
641	*Zephaniah*	JOSIAH			
610	*Obadiah?*	JEHOAHAZ	*Habakkuk*		
609	*Joel?*	JEHOIAKIM			
598	*Jeremiah*	JECONIAH			
597	*Daniel*	ZEDEKIAH	*Ezekiel*		
586					

BABYLONIAN CAPTIVITY   *Haggai (520)   Zechariah (520)*

538

Joel?   MEDO PERSIAN RULE   *Malachi (458-420)   Jonah?*

330

To your tents, O Israel!

Now look to your own house, David!"

Then all the Israelites went home, ¹⁷ but Rehoboam *still* ruled over the Israelites who lived in the cities of Judah.

¹⁸ King Rehoboam sent messengers to Hadoram,*ᵃ* who was in charge of the forced labor, but the *Northern* Israelites stoned him with stones, and he died. King Rehoboam hastily mounted his chariot and fled to Jerusalem. ¹⁹ So *Northern* Israel has been in rebellion against the house of David to this day.

Rehoboam Regains Some Control

¹ Rehoboam went to Jerusalem and assembled the houses of Judah and Benjamin—180,000 choice warriors—to fight against *Northern* Israel and return the kingdom to himself. ² But the word of the LORD came to Shemaiah the man of God, saying, ³ "Speak to Rehoboam son of Solomon, king of Israel, and to all Judah and Benjamin*ᵇ* and say, ⁴ 'The LORD says this: Do not go up and fight with your relatives. Everyone return home, for this situation is from me.'" They listened to the words of the LORD and turned back from going against Jeroboam.

⁵ Rehoboam stayed in Jerusalem and built fortified cities in Judah. ⁶ He built up

Bethlehem,	Adullam,	Lachish,
Etam,	Gath, ⁸	Azekah,
Tekoa,	Mareshah,	Zorah, ¹⁰
Beth-Zur, ⁷	Ziph,	Aijalon, and
Soco,	Adoraim, ⁹	Hebron.

These were the fortified cities in Judah and Benjamin. ¹¹ He strengthened their defenses and put officers in them, along with storehouses of food, oil, and wine. ¹² He furnished every city with large shields and lances *for their garrisons* and made them extremely strong. Thus Judah and Benjamin were his.

¹³ The priests and Levites who were in all the *territory* of Israel took their stand *against Jeroboam* from all their districts. ¹⁴ The Levites abandoned their pasturelands and property and relocated to Judah and Jerusalem, because Jeroboam and his sons had rejected them from serving as priests to the LORD. ¹⁵ He set up his own priests at the high-place shrines for the goat and calf idols he had made. ¹⁶ After that, people from every tribe in Israel followed them, *people* who gave their hearts to seek the LORD, the God of Israel. They came to Jerusalem to sacrifice to the LORD, the God of their ancestors. ¹⁷ For three years they made the kingdom of Judah strong and supported Rehoboam son of Solomon. *This was because* they walked in the ways of David and Solomon for three years.

---

a "Hadoram": a variant spelling of Adoniram.
b From the Septuagint; Masoretic text: "to all Israel in Judah and Benjamin."

Genealogy of Rehoboam

[18] Rehoboam took a wife *for himself.*

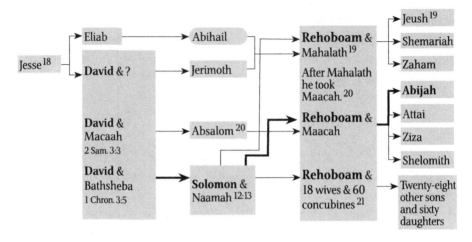

[22] He appointed Abijah son of Maacah to be head and leader over his brothers, for he intended to make him king.

[21] Rehoboam loved Maacah daughter of Absalom more than all his *other* wives or concubines (he had eighteen wives and sixty concubines, who bore him twenty-eight sons and sixty daughters). [23] Rehoboam acted wisely when he dispersed some of his sons throughout the districts of Judah and Benjamin to all the fortified cities. He gave them abundant provisions and sought many wives for them.

12 *2 Chronicles*

Egypt Captures Judah and Jerusalem

[1] When Rehoboam's kingdom was established and he had become strong, he and all Israel abandoned the Law of the Lord. [2] Because they had rebelled against the Lord, in the fifth year of King Rehoboam, Shishak king of Egypt went up against Jerusalem [3] with twelve hundred chariots, sixty thousand horsemen, and innumerable hordes who went with him from Egypt—Libyans, Sukkites,[a] and Cushites. [4] He captured the fortified cities of Judah and went as far as Jerusalem.

[5] Then Shemaiah the prophet went to Rehoboam and the princes of Judah who were gathered in Jerusalem because of Shishak. He told them, "The Lord says this: 'You have abandoned me, so I have abandoned you to the hand of Shishak.'"

[6] The princes of Judah and the king humbled themselves and said, "The Lord is righteous."

[7] When the Lord saw that they had humbled themselves, the word of the Lord *came* to Shemaiah, saying, "They have humbled themselves. I will not destroy them, but I will give them a partial rescue after a while. My wrath will not be poured out on Jerusalem by the hand of Shishak, [8] but they will be slaves to him. Then they will know *the difference between* serving me and serving the kingdoms of the lands."

---

a "Sukkites": Africans about whom nothing is known beyond what is stated in this verse.

⁹ Then Shishak king of Egypt went up against Jerusalem and took the treasures of the temple of the Lᴏʀᴅ and the treasures of the palace; he took everything. He took all the golden shields that Solomon had made. ¹⁰ King Rehoboam made bronze shields in their place and put them in the care of the captains of the guard who guarded the doors to the palace. ¹¹ Whenever the king went to the temple of the Lᴏʀᴅ, the guards would bring them out and then return them to the guardroom. ¹² Because Rehoboam humbled himself, the wrath of the Lᴏʀᴅ turned from him, and he did not destroy him completely. There were yet *some* good things in Judah.

¹³ Rehoboam strengthened himself in Jerusalem and reigned. He was forty-one years old when he became king, and he reigned for seventeen years in Jerusalem, the city from among all the tribes of Israel in which the Lᴏʀᴅ had chosen to put his name. Rehoboam's mother's name was Naamah the Ammonite. ¹⁴ He did evil, for he did not set his heart on seeking the Lᴏʀᴅ.

¹⁵ The acts of Rehoboam, from beginning to end, are written in the records*ᵃ* of Shemaiah the prophet and Iddo the seer. There was continual*ᵇ* war between Rehoboam and Jeroboam. ¹⁶ Rehoboam lay down with his ancestors and was buried in the City of David, and his son Abijah reigned in his place.

2 Chronicles **13**

Abijah's Reign over Judah

¹ Abijah began to reign over Judah in the eighteenth year of King Jeroboam. ² He reigned for three years in Jerusalem. His mother's name was Maacah*ᶜ* daughter of Uriel from Gibeah.

Now there was war between Abijah and Jeroboam. ³ Abijah mustered four hundred thousand warriors for the army, choice men. Jeroboam arranged his people for battle: eight hundred thousand warriors, *also* choice men. ⁴ Then Abijah got up *to speak* on Mount Zemaraim, which is in the hill country of Ephraim, and said,

"Listen to me, Jeroboam and all *Northern* Israel! ⁵ Do you not know that the Lᴏʀᴅ, the God of Israel, gave the kingdom of Israel to David and his descendants forever by a covenant of salt? ⁶ But Jeroboam son of Nebat, a servant of Solomon son of David, rose up and rebelled against his master. ⁷ Some worthless men, scoundrels,*ᵈ* gathered around him and were too strong for Rehoboam son of Solomon when he was an indecisive youth and not strong enough to resist them. ⁸ Now you are talking about strengthening yourselves *for war* before the kingdom of the Lᴏʀᴅ, *which is* in the hand of the sons of David—you, a great multitude with golden calves that Jeroboam made for you as gods! ⁹ Didn't you drive out the priests of the Lᴏʀᴅ, the descendants of Aaron and the Levites, and make yourselves priests like *those of* the peoples of *the other* lands? *For you,* anyone who comes to consecrate himself*ᵉ* with a young bull and seven rams may be a priest of *what are idols,* not gods!

---

a Literally, "the words."
b Literally, "all their days."
c From the Septuagint; Masoretic text: "Micaiah."
d Literally, "sons of Belial."
e Literally, "to fill his hand."

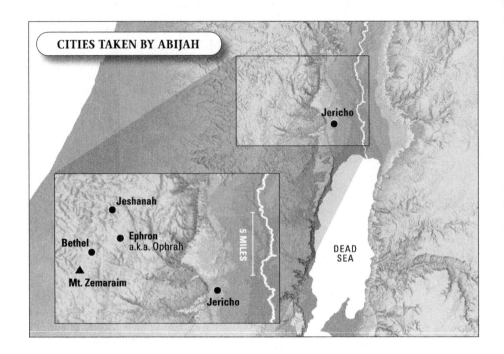

[Map labels: Jericho; Jeshanah; Bethel; Ephron a.k.a. Ophrah; Mt. Zemaraim; Jericho; 5 MILES; DEAD SEA]

[10] "But we *follow* the Lᴏʀᴅ our God and have not abandoned him. And the priests who minister before the Lᴏʀᴅ are the descendants of Aaron, and the Levites assist them. [11] They offer fragrant[a] incense and burnt offerings to the Lᴏʀᴅ every morning and evening. They set out the showbread on the ceremonially clean table and light *the* lamps in the golden lampstand every evening. We are keeping the charge of the Lᴏʀᴅ our God, but you have abandoned him! [12] Look, God is with us at our head, and his priests will blow trumpets to sound the battle cry against you. People of Israel, do not fight against the Lᴏʀᴅ, the God of your ancestors, for you will not succeed."

[13] But Jeroboam had gone around to bring an ambush from behind *Abijah's army. The main force* was in front of *the men of* Judah, and the ambush was behind them. [14] When *the army of* Judah looked around, to their surprise, the battle was in front of them and behind them! They cried out to the Lᴏʀᴅ, and the priests blew the trumpets. [15] The men of Judah raised the battle cry. When they did, God struck Jeroboam and all *the Northern* Israel *army* before Abijah and Judah. [16] The *Northern* Israelites fled before Judah, and God delivered them into their hand. [17] Abijah and his people struck them with a huge slaughter. Five hundred thousand choice troops from *Northern* Israel fell slain. [18] The *Northern* Israelite *army* was subdued at that time, and the Judahite *army* became strong because they relied on the Lᴏʀᴅ, the God of their ancestors. [19] Abijah pursued Jeroboam and captured cities from him: Bethel and its villages, Jeshanah and its villages, and Ephron and its villages.

---

a   Literally, "spice."

86

²⁰Jeroboam did not regain strength in the days of Abijah. The Lᴏʀᴅ struck him and he died. ²¹ But Abijah grew in strength and took fourteen wives and had twenty-two sons and sixteen daughters.

²² The rest of the acts of Abijah, his ways and his words, are recorded in the History of the Prophet Iddo. ¹⁴:¹ᵃ Abijah lay down with his ancestors, and they buried him in the City of David. His son Asa reigned in his place.

2 Chronicles **14**

Good King Asa's Reign over Judah

¹ᵇ In Asa's time the land rested *from war* for ten years. ² Asa did what was good and right in the eyes of the Lᴏʀᴅ his God. ³ He removed the foreign altars and the high-place shrines, smashed the idols,ᵃ and cut down the Asherah poles. ⁴ He ordered Judah to seek the Lᴏʀᴅ, the God of their ancestors, and to obey the Law and the commandment. ⁵ He removed the high-place shrines and incense altars from all the cities of Judah, and the kingdom experienced peace under him. ⁶ He built fortified cities in Judah, for the land was at peace; he had no wars in those years. The Lᴏʀᴅ gave him rest. ⁷ Asa said to Judah, "Let's build these cities and surround them with walls, towers, and gates with bars. The land is still ours because we have sought the Lᴏʀᴅ our God. We have sought him, and he has given us rest on every side." So they built and prospered.

Asa Defeats Zerah

⁸ Asa had an army of 300,000 *troops* from Judah, armed with large shields and spears, and 280,000 from Benjamin, carrying small shields and armed with bows.

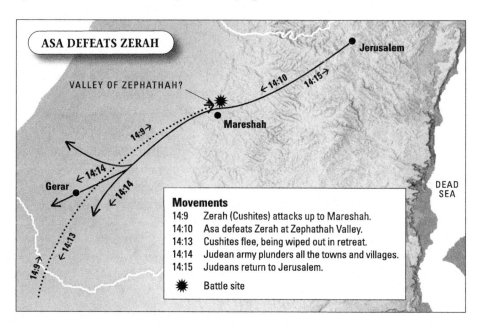

ASA DEFEATS ZERAH

Jerusalem

VALLEY OF ZEPHATHAH?

14:10

14:15

14:9

Mareshah

14:14

Gerar

14:14

14:13

14:9

DEAD SEA

Movements
14:9   Zerah (Cushites) attacks up to Mareshah.
14:10   Asa defeats Zerah at Zephathah Valley.
14:13   Cushites flee, being wiped out in retreat.
14:14   Judean army plunders all the towns and villages.
14:15   Judeans return to Jerusalem.
✸   Battle site

a Literally, "sacred pillars."

All of them were brave warriors. [9] Zerah the Cushite attacked them with an army of countless thousands[a] and three hundred chariots, advancing as far as Mareshah. [10] Asa went out to face him and arranged his *troops* for battle in the Zephathah Valley near Mareshah. [11] Asa called upon the LORD his God and said,

> "O LORD, there is none like you to help the powerless against the mighty. Help us, O LORD our God, for we rely on you and have come out against this multitude in your name. O LORD, you are our God; do not let *mere* mortals prevail against you."

[12] So the LORD defeated the Cushites before Asa and Judah, and they fled.

[13] Asa and the people who were with him pursued them all the way to Gerar. The Cushites fell until there were none left alive, for they were shattered before the LORD and his army.[b] *The men of Judah* carried away a tremendous amount of plunder. [14] They defeated all the towns around Gerar, for the terror of the LORD was on them. They plundered all the villages, because there was much plunder in them. [15] They also struck the herdsmen camps[c] and captured large numbers of sheep and camels. Then they returned to Jerusalem.

15 *2 Chronicles*

Asa's Reforms

[1] The Spirit of God came on Azariah son of Oded. [2] And he went out to face Asa and said to him,

> "Listen to me, Asa and all Judah and Benjamin! The LORD is with you when you are with him. If you seek him, he will be found by you. But if you abandon him, he will abandon you. [3] For a long time Israel was without the true God, without a priest who teaches, and without *God's* law. [4] But in their distress they turned to the LORD, the God of Israel, and sought him, and he was found by them. [5] In those times there was no peace for anyone,[d] because many troubles were upon the inhabitants of the lands. [6] Nation was destroyed by nation and city *destroyed* by city, for God has troubled them with every kind of adversity. [7] But you, be strong and do not let your hands be weak, for your work will be rewarded."

[8] When Asa heard these words, the prophecy of Azariah the prophet, he took courage and removed all the detestable idols from all the land of Judah and Benjamin and from the cities he had captured in the hills of Ephraim. He refurbished the altar of the LORD that was in the front of the court of *the house of* the LORD. [9] He assembled all Judah and Benjamin and all who were staying with them from *the territories of* Ephraim, Manasseh, and Simeon, for many from *the tribes of Northern* Israel came over to him when they saw that the LORD his God was with him. [10] They assembled in Jerusalem in the third month in the fifteenth year of Asa's reign. [11] They sacrificed to the LORD that day out of the plunder they had brought:

---

a Literally, "a thousand thousands." The Hebrew syntax suggests an interpretation of "a superlative thousand" or "a number too great to be counted."
b Literally, "his camp."
c Literally, "livestock camps."
d Literally, "for those who went out or came in."

seven hundred oxen and seven thousand sheep. [12] And they entered into a covenant to seek the Lord, the God of their ancestors, with all their hearts and all their souls. [13] Anyone who did not seek the Lord, the God of Israel, was put to death, whether small or great,[a] man or woman. [14] They made their pledge to the Lord with a loud voice, shouting, and with *the sound of* trumpets and ram's horns. [15] All Judah rejoiced in their pledge, because they had sworn it with all their hearts and sought God with all their desire. And he was found by them, and the Lord gave them rest on every side.

[16] King Asa removed his grandmother Maacah *from her office* as queen mother, because she had made an Asherah pole, a horrible idol. Asa cut it down, crushed it to bits, and burned it in the Kidron Valley. [17] Although he did not remove the high-place shrines from Israel, Asa's heart was complete*ly committed* all his days. [18] He brought into the temple of God the things that his father had dedicated *to God* and that he had dedicated: silver and gold and utensils. [19] And there was no more war until the thirty-fifth year of Asa's reign.

2 Chronicles **16**

Asa and Ben-Hadad Defeat Northern Israel

See map on next page

[1] In the thirty-sixth year of Asa's reign, Baasha king of *Northern* Israel went up against Judah and built *fortifications at* Ramah so that no one could come in or go out to *the territory of* Asa king of Judah. [2] So Asa brought out silver and gold from the treasuries in the temple of the Lord and the palace and sent it to Ben-Hadad, the king of Aram who lived in Damascus, saying, [3] *"Let there be* a treaty between you and me, *as there was* between my father and your father. Look, I have sent you silver and gold. Break your treaty with Baasha the king of *Northern* Israel so he will withdraw *his forces* from me."

[4] Ben-Hadad listened to King Asa and sent his army commanders against the cities of *Northern* Israel. They conquered Ijon, Dan, Abel Maim, and all the storage cities of Naphtali. [5] When Baasha heard *of this,* he stopped fortifying Ramah and ceased his *other* work *there.* [6] Then King Asa took all Judah to fetch the stones and timber from Ramah with which Baasha had been building. He built Geba and Mizpah with them.

Death of Asa

[7] At that time Hanani the prophet came to Asa king of Judah and said to him, "Because you relied on the king of Aram and not on the Lord your God, the army of the king of Aram has escaped out of your hand. [8] Weren't the Cushites and Libyans a massive army, with vast numbers of chariots and cavalry? Yet when you relied on the Lord, he gave them into your hand. [9] The eyes of the Lord range about throughout the whole earth, that he may strongly support those who are wholeheartedly devoted to him. You have acted foolishly in this matter; therefore from now on you will be at war." [10] Then Asa was angry with the prophet, so he put him in prison. He was enraged about this *prophecy.* And Asa oppressed some of the people at that time.

---

a Or "young or old."

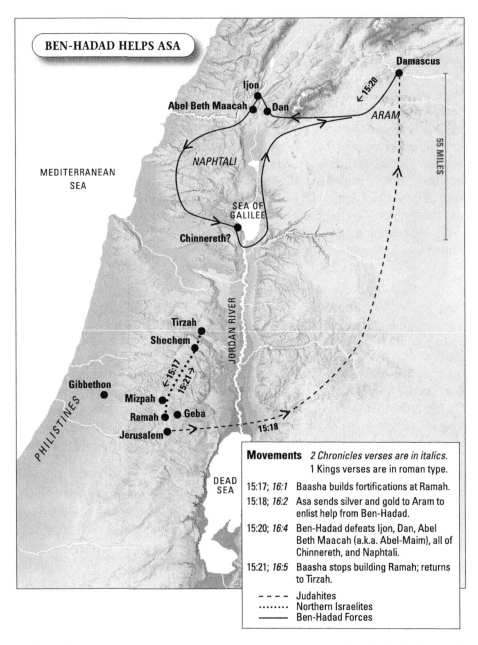

BEN-HADAD HELPS ASA

Damascus

Ijon

Abel Beth Maacah Dan

ARAM

←15:20

55 MILES

NAPHTALI

MEDITERRANEAN
SEA

SEA OF
GALILEE

Chinnereth?

JORDAN RIVER

Tirzah

Shechem

←15:17→
15:21→

Gibbethon

Mizpah

Ramah Geba

Jerusalem

15:18

DEAD
SEA

Movements *2 Chronicles verses are in italics.*
1 Kings verses are in roman type.

15:17; *16:1* Baasha builds fortifications at Ramah.

15:18; *16:2* Asa sends silver and gold to Aram to
enlist help from Ben-Hadad.

15:20; *16:4* Ben-Hadad defeats Ijon, Dan, Abel
Beth Maacah (a.k.a. Abel-Maim), all of
Chinnereth, and Naphtali.

15:21; *16:5* Baasha stops building Ramah; returns
to Tirzah.

- - - - Judahites
.... Northern Israelites
——— Ben-Hadad Forces

[11] Look, the acts of Asa, from beginning to end, are recorded in the book Kings of Judah and Israel. [12] In the thirty-ninth year of his reign, Asa contracted a disease in his feet until it became very severe. Even in his illness he did not seek *help* from the LORD, but *only sought help* from the physicians. [13] Asa lay down with his ancestors in the forty-first year of his reign. [14] They buried him in the tomb he had hewn out for himself in the City of David. They laid him on a bier filled with spices and various mixtures (*i.e.*, blended perfumes) and made a huge fire in his honor.[a]

---

a Literally, "for him."

Jehoshaphat's Righteous Reign over Judah

[1] His son Jehoshaphat reigned in his place and strengthened himself against *Northern* Israel. [2] He put troops in all the fortified cities of Judah and put garrisons in the land of Judah and the cities of Ephraim that his father Asa had captured. [3] The LORD was with Jehoshaphat because he walked in the ways of his ancestor David from the beginning *of his reign* and did not seek the Baals. [4] He sought the God of his father and walked according to his commandments, not acting like *Northern* Israel. [5] The LORD established the kingdom in his hand, and all Judah brought tribute to Jehoshaphat. He had great wealth and honor. [6] His heart took delight in the ways of the LORD, and he again removed the high-place shrines and Asherah poles from Judah.

[7] In the third year of his reign, he sent his officials (*i.e.,* Ben-Hail, Zechariah, Obadiah, Nethanel, and Micaiah) to teach in the cities of Judah. [8] *He sent* with them the Levites

Shemaiah,	Shemiramoth,	Tob-Adonijah;
Nethaniah,	Jehonathan,	and with them the priests,
Zebadiah,	Adonijah, and	Elishama and
Asahel,	Tobijah,	Jehoram.

[9] And they taught in Judah. They had the book of the Law of the LORD with them, and they circulated through all the cities of Judah and taught among the people.

[10] Then the terror of the LORD fell upon all the kingdoms of the lands surrounding Judah, so none of them would fight with Jehoshaphat. [11] Some of the Philistines sent him a gift and silver as tribute. And the Arabs too brought him flocks of 7,700 rams and 7,700 male goats.

[12] So Jehoshaphat became very great and built fortresses and store cities in Judah. [13] He had large supplies in the cities of Judah and soldiers, mighty men of valor in Jerusalem.

Registry of Troops [17:14-19]

[14a] This was their registry by families. [19] These were *the warriors* that served the king, as well as those he stationed in the fortified cities throughout Judah.

Commanders of Thousands	Troops
From Judah	
Adnah, commander in chief [14b]	300,000
Jehohanan, commander [15]	280,000
Amasiah son of Zicri [16] He volunteered for the LORD's *service.*	200,000
From Benjamin [17]	
Eliada A brave warrior	200,000 troops armed with bows and shields
Jehozabad [18]	180,000 troops armed for war

Jehoshaphat Follows False Prophets

[1] Jehoshaphat had great wealth and honor, and by marriage became related to Ahab. [2] After some years, he went down to Ahab at Samaria. Ahab slaughtered large numbers of sheep and cattle for him and the people with him, and persuaded him to go up to fight against Ramoth Gilead. [3] Ahab king of *Northern* Israel asked Jehoshaphat king of Judah, "Will you go with me to *recover* Ramoth Gilead *from Aram*?"

Jehoshaphat replied, "I am as you are, and my army as your army. We will be with you in the battle." [4] But Jehoshaphat also said to the king of *Northern* Israel, "*But first,* today, seek the word of the Lord."

[5] So the king of *Northern* Israel assembled the prophets, four hundred of them, and asked them, "Should we go to Ramoth Gilead to fight, or should I refrain?"

They replied, "Go ahead; God will put *it* into the king's hand."

[6] But Jehoshaphat said, "Isn't there still a prophet of the Lord here, so we can ask him?"

[7] The king of *Northern* Israel replied, "There's still one man through whom we can ask the Lord a question, Micaiah son of Imlah. But I hate him because he never prophesies good *things* for me, but always bad *things*."

Jehoshaphat said, "The king shouldn't speak like that."

[8] The king of *Northern* Israel summoned a high official and said, "Bring Micaiah son of Imlah quickly."

[9] *Later,* the king of *Northern* Israel and Jehoshaphat king of Judah were each sitting on their thrones, dressed in their *royal* robes, seated at the threshing floor by the entrance at the gate of Samaria. All the prophets were prophesying before them. [10] Zedekiah son of Kenaanah had made himself iron horns and said, "The Lord says this: 'With these you will gore the Arameans until they are destroyed.'"

[11] All the *other* prophets were prophesying similarly, saying, "Go up to Ramoth Gilead and you'll find success; the Lord will put it into the king's hand."

[12] The messenger who went to summon Micaiah said to him, "Look, the prophets are *like* one mouth *speaking*—pleasing the king. Now please let your word be like one of theirs and speak agreeably."

[13] But Micaiah replied, "As the Lord lives, whatever my God says I will say."

[14] He went to the king, and the king asked him, "Micaiah, should we go to war against Ramoth Gilead, or should I refrain?"

Micaiah said, "Go up and you'll find success; they'll be put into your hands."

[15] But the king said to him, "How many times must I make you swear to say nothing to me except the truth in the name of the Lord?"

[16] Micaiah replied, "I saw all *Northern* Israel scattered on the mountains like sheep without a shepherd. The Lord said, 'These have no master. Let each one return home in peace.'"

¹⁷ Then the king of *Northern* Israel said to Jehoshaphat, "Didn't I tell you that he never prophesies good things for me, but only bad?"

¹⁸ And Micaiah said, "Listen to the word of the LORD:

'I saw the LORD seated on his throne. All the army of heaven was standing on his right and his left. ¹⁹ The LORD asked, "Who will lure Ahab king of Israel so that he will go up and fall *slain* at Ramoth Gilead?"

'This one said this, and another one said that. ²⁰ Then a certain spirit came forward and stood before the LORD. He said, "I'll lure him."

'The LORD asked him, "How?"

²¹ 'He replied, "I'll go out and be a lying spirit in the mouths of all his prophets."

'*The* LORD said, "You will lure him. You'll lure him and succeed. Go and do it."'"

²² *Micaiah continued,* "And now, look, the LORD has put a lying spirit in the mouths of these prophets of yours. The LORD has decreed disaster for you!"

²³ Then Zedekiah son of Kenaanah approached Micaiah and struck him on the cheek,ᵃ saying, "Which way did the spirit from the LORD go when it went from me to speak to you?"

²⁴ Micaiah said, "Look, you'll see on that day when you hide in an inner room."

²⁵ Then the king of *Northern* Israel ordered, "Seize Micaiah and return him to Amon the city ruler and to Joash the king's son. ²⁶ Tell them, 'The king says this: Put this one in prison. Feed him only a little bread and waterᵇ until I return safely.'"

²⁷ Micaiah said, "If you ever return safely, then the LORD has not spoken through me." And he added, "Listen *well,* all you people!"

²⁸ Then the king of *Northern* Israel and Jehoshaphat king of Judah went up to *fight Aram at* Ramoth Gilead. ²⁹ The king of *Northern* Israel said to Jehoshaphat, "I'll disguise myself and go into battle, but you dress in your *royal* robes." So the king of *Northern* Israel disguised himself, and they went into battle.

³⁰ The king of Aram had commanded his chariot officers, "Don't fight with anyone small or great except the king of *Northern* Israel alone."

³¹ When the chariot officers saw Jehoshaphat, they said *to one another,* "It's the king of *Northern* Israel!" And they turned to attack him, but Jehoshaphat cried out and the LORD helped him; God drew them away from him.

³² When the chariot officers realized he was not the king of *Northern* Israel, they turned away from pursuing him. ³³ But someone shot his bow randomly and hit the king of *Northern* Israel in a joint of his armor!

Ahab ordered his chariot driver, "Turn aroundᶜ and get me out of the fight. I'm wounded."

³⁴ The battle raged all that day. And the king of *Northern* Israel was propped up in his chariot, facing the Arameans until evening, and he died at sunset.

---

a A slap was a terrible insult, declaring the victim as worthy of contempt.
b Literally, "only bread of affliction and water of affliction."
c Literally, "Turn your hand."

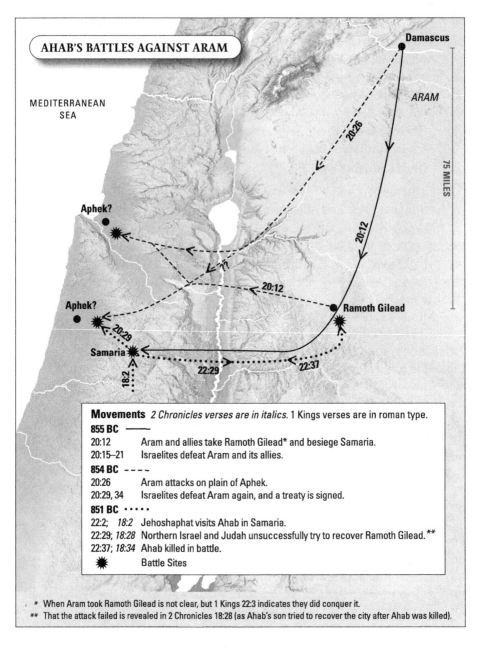

AHAB'S BATTLES AGAINST ARAM

Damascus

MEDITERRANEAN
SEA

ARAM

75 MILES

20:26

20:12

Aphek?

?

20:12

Aphek?

Ramoth Gilead

20:29

Samaria

22:29

22:37

18:2

Movements *2 Chronicles verses are in italics.* 1 Kings verses are in roman type.

855 BC ——
20:12 Aram and allies take Ramoth Gilead* and besiege Samaria.
20:15–21 Israelites defeat Aram and its allies.

854 BC - - - -
20:26 Aram attacks on plain of Aphek.
20:29, 34 Israelites defeat Aram again, and a treaty is signed.

851 BC · · · · ·
22:2; *18:2* Jehoshaphat visits Ahab in Samaria.
22:29; *18:28* Northern Israel and Judah unsuccessfully try to recover Ramoth Gilead. **
22:37; *18:34* Ahab killed in battle.
✹ Battle Sites

* When Aram took Ramoth Gilead is not clear, but 1 Kings 22:3 indicates they did conquer it.
** That the attack failed is revealed in 2 Chronicles 18:28 (as Ahab's son tried to recover the city after Ahab was killed).

19 *2 Chronicles*

Jehoshaphat Returns to God

[1] Jehoshaphat king of Judah returned to his palace in Jerusalem safely. [2] But Jehu the prophet, son of Hanani, went out to meet him[a] and said to him, "Should you help the wicked and love those who hate the LORD? The LORD's anger is upon you because of

---

a Literally, "went out before him."

this! ³ Nevertheless, there are some good things found in you. You have burned the Asherah poles in Judah and have set your heart on seeking God."

⁴ Jehoshaphat lived in Jerusalem. He went out again among the people from Beersheba to the hill country of Ephraim and turned them back to the Lᴏʀᴅ, the God of their ancestors. ⁵ He appointed judges in the land and in all the fortified cities of Judah, city by city. ⁶ He said to them, "Consider what you are doing. You are not judging for man but for the Lᴏʀᴅ; he is with you giving the verdict. ⁷ Now may the fear of the Lᴏʀᴅ be upon you. Keep *his commands* and do *them,* for with the Lᴏʀᴅ our God there is no injustice, partiality, or bribery."

⁸ In Jerusalem, Jehoshaphat also appointed some Levites, priests, and Israelite family leaders for *pronouncing* the judgment of the Lᴏʀᴅ and to settle disputes among the inhabitants of Jerusalem. ⁹ He charged them, saying, "This is what you are to do in the fear of the Lᴏʀᴅ, faithfully and wholeheartedly. ¹⁰ Whatever lawsuit comes before you from your relatives who live in their cities—whether it pertains to bloodshed, Law,ᵃ commandments, statutes, or ordinances—you shall warn them so that they may not incur guilt before the Lᴏʀᴅ, and wrath will not come upon you and your relatives. Do this, and you will not incur guilt.

¹¹ Look,

Amariah the chief priest
    will be over you in all matters *pertaining to* the Lᴏʀᴅ, and
Zebadiah son of Ishmael, the leader of the tribe of Judah,
    will be over you in all matters *pertaining to* the king.
The Levites
    will also serve as officials before you.

Be strong and do it, and may the Lᴏʀᴅ be with those *who do* well."

2 Chronicles 20

Jehoshaphat's Prayer and Victories

¹ After this, the Moabites and Ammonites and some of the Meunitesᵇ came to battle against Jehoshaphat. ² *Messengers* came to Jehoshaphat and told him, "A huge horde is coming up against you from across the Dead Sea, out of Edom.ᶜ Look, it's *already* in Hazazon Tamar (i.e., En Gedi)." ³ Jehoshaphat was afraid. So he set his face to seek the Lᴏʀᴅ, and he proclaimed a fast for all Judah. ⁴ Judah gathered together to seek the Lᴏʀᴅ; indeed, *people* from all the cities of Judah came to seek the Lᴏʀᴅ.

⁵ Jehoshaphat stood in the assembly of Judah and Jerusalem at the temple of the Lᴏʀᴅ in front of the new courtyard ⁶ and said,

"O Lᴏʀᴅ, God of our ancestors, are you not God in heaven? You rule over all the kingdoms of the nations. Strength and power are in your hand, and no one can stand against you. ⁷ Aren't you our God who drove out the inhabitants of this land before your people Israel and gave it to the descendants of your friend

---

a Literally, "whether between blood, between Law."
b From the Septuagint; Masoretic text: "some of the Ammonites."
c Literally, "out of Aram." But in light of verses 10 and 22, this appears to be a copyist error.

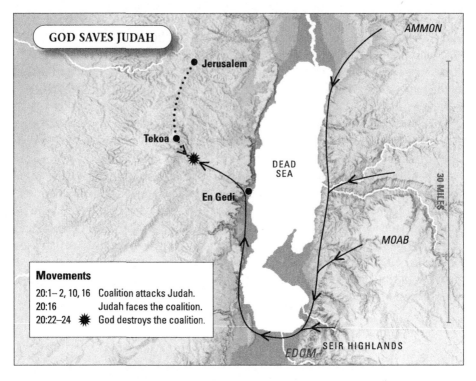

GOD SAVES JUDAH

AMMON

Jerusalem

Tekoa

DEAD
SEA

En Gedi

MOAB

30 MILES

Movements

20:1–2, 10, 16   Coalition attacks Judah.
20:16   Judah faces the coalition.
20:22–24 ✸   God destroys the coalition.

EDOM   SEIR HIGHLANDS

Abraham forever? [8] They lived in it and have built you a sanctuary in it for your name, saying, [9] 'If disaster comes upon us, *whether* the sword of judgment or plague or famine, let us stand *praying* before you and this temple, for your name is in this temple. Let us cry out to you in our distress. You will hear us and rescue us!'

[10] "Now look! The Ammonites, Moabites, and people from the Seir highlands, whom you did not allow Israel to invade when they came from the land of Egypt (the Israelites turned aside from them and did not destroy them)—[11] see how they are repaying us by coming to drive us out of the inheritance you gave us. [12] Our God, will you not execute judgment upon them? We have no strength before this huge horde that is coming against us. We do not know what to do, but our eyes are upon you."

[13] All Judah was standing there before the Lord with their infants, wives, and children. [14] Then, in the midst of the assembly, the Spirit of the Lord came upon Jahaziel son of Zechariah, son of Benaiah, son of Jeiel, son of Mattaniah, a Levite from the descendants of Asaph. [15] He said,

"Listen well, all Judah, inhabitants of Jerusalem, and King Jehoshaphat! The Lord says this to you:

'Do not fear or be terrified before this huge horde.

The battle is God's, not yours.

¹⁶ Go down against them tomorrow.

> Look, they will be climbing up via the Pass of Ziz. You will find them at
> the end of the gorge in front of the Wilderness of Jeruel. ¹⁷ You will not
> have to fight them at this *time.*

Take your stand

> and see the victory of the Lord on behalf of Judah and Jerusalem.

Do not be afraid and dismayed.

Go out before them tomorrow,

> and the Lord will be with you.'"

¹⁸ Jehoshaphat bowed his head with his face to the ground. And all Judah and
the inhabitants of Jerusalem fell down before the Lord, worshiping the Lord. ¹⁹ The
Levites *from the clans* of the Kohathites and Korahites rose up to praise the Lord God
of Israel with a very loud voice.

²⁰ *The next day* they got up early in the morning and went out to the Wilderness
of Tekoa. When they left, Jehoshaphat stood and said, "Listen to me, Judah and
residents of Jerusalem! Trust in the Lord your God, and you will be upheld; trust in his
prophets, and you will succeed!"

²¹ He consulted with the people and appointed singers to the Lord, those who
praise him in holy attire. As they went out before the army, they were saying, "Give
thanks to the Lord, for his loyal love is forever." ²² The moment they began to praise
and shout,^a the Lord set ambushes against the troops of Ammon, Moab, and the
Seir highlands who were invading Judah, and they were crushed. ²³ The Ammonites
and Moabites rose up against the troops from the Seir highlands to destroy and
annihilate them! When they had finished with the troops from the Seir highlands,
they helped *Judah by* destroying each other.

²⁴ Judah came to the outlook point over the wilderness and looked toward the
horde. To their surprise, they saw *nothing but* corpses fallen on the ground; not one
had escaped! ²⁵ When Jehoshaphat and his army went to take their plunder, they
found a huge amount among the corpses: equipment, clothing, and valuables on
them. They took for themselves more than they could carry. They took three days
to collect all the plunder because there was so much. ²⁶ On the fourth day they
assembled in the Valley of Beracah (*i.e.,* Valley of Blessing), for they blessed the Lord
there. Therefore it has been named the Valley of Beracah until today.

²⁷ With Jehoshaphat at their head, all the men of Judah and Jerusalem returned
to Jerusalem with joy, for the Lord had made possible their rejoicing over their
enemies. ²⁸ And they entered Jerusalem *and went* to the temple of the Lord *playing*
harps, lyres, and trumpets. ²⁹ And the fear of God was upon all the surrounding
kingdoms when they heard that the Lord had fought against Israel's enemies.
³⁰ Then Jehoshaphat's kingdom was at peace, for his God gave him rest on every side.

³¹ So Jehoshaphat was *king* over Judah. He was thirty-five years old when he
began to reign, and he reigned for twenty-five years in Jerusalem. His mother's name
was Azubah daughter of Shilhi. ³² He walked in the way of his father Asa and did
not turn from doing *what was* right in the eyes of the Lord, ³³ except that he did not

---

a   Or "began to sing and praise."

remove the high-place shrines. For the people had still not set their hearts on the God of their ancestors. ³⁴ The rest of the matters regarding Jehoshaphat, from beginning to end—take a look, they're recorded in the Words of Jehu Son of Hanani, which is included in the book Kings of Israel.

³⁵ After this Jehoshaphat king of Judah allied himself with Ahaziah king of *Northern* Israel who acted wickedly. ³⁶ They made an alliance to build trading ships, and they made them at Ezion Geber. ³⁷ Then Eliezer son of Dodavahu from Mareshah prophesied to Jehoshaphat, saying, "Because you allied yourself with Ahaziah, the LORD will burst forth against your works." Then the ships were wrecked and not able to go to Tarshish.

21 *2 Chronicles*

Jehoram's Evil Reign over Judah

¹ Jehoshaphat lay down with his ancestors and was buried with them in the City of David. His son Jehoram reigned in his place.

² Jehoram had brothers: Azariah, Jehiel, Zechariah, Azariahu,*ᵃ* Michael, and Shephatiah. All these were sons of Jehoshaphat king of Israel. ³ Their father gave them many gifts of silver, gold, and precious things, as well as fortified cities in Judah, but he gave the kingdom to Jehoram because he was the firstborn. ⁴ And when Jehoram was established over his father's kingdom, he became ruthless, murdering all his brothers and even some of the officials of Israel with the sword.

⁵ Jehoram was thirty-two years old when he became king, and he reigned for eight years in Jerusalem. ⁶ He walked in the ways of the kings of *Northern* Israel, just as Ahab's family had done, for Ahab's daughter was his wife. He did evil in the eyes of the LORD. ⁷ But the LORD was not willing to wipe out the family of David, because of the covenant he had made with David, since he had promised to give a lamp to him and his descendants forever.

Edom's Successful Rebellion

⁸ In Jehoram's days Edom rebelled from being under the hand of Judah and crowned their own king. ⁹ Jehoram, his officers, and all his chariots crossed *the border*. He and his chariot officers got up at night and broke through the Edomites who were surrounding him. ¹⁰ So Edom has been in rebellion against the authority*ᵇ* of Judah to this day.

Then at the same time Libnah rebelled against Jehoram's rule,*ᶜ* for he had forsaken the LORD, the God of his ancestors. ¹¹ He also made high-place shrines in the hill country of Judah, causing the inhabitants of Jerusalem to prostitute themselves, and leading Judah astray.

---

a Or "*another* Azariah."
b Literally, "the hand."
c Literally, "hand."

¹² A letter came to him from Elijah the prophet,ᵃ saying,

> To: Jehoram
>
> From: Elijah the prophet
>
> The LORD God of your ancestor David says this:
>> You have not walked in the ways of your father Jehoshaphat and *your grandfather* Asa king of Judah, ¹³ but
>>
>> *you have walked* in the way of the kings of *Northern* Israel, leading Judah and the residents of Jerusalem to prostitute themselves, just like Ahab's family prostituted themselves, even murdering your brothers, members of your own family, who were better men than you.
>
> ¹⁴ Therefore look out!
>> The LORD is about to strike your people, your sons, your wives, and everything you own with a great blow.
>> ¹⁵ You will become terribly sick with a disease of the intestines, such that your bowels will come out day after day.

¹⁶ Then the LORD stirred up the spirit of the Philistines and the Arabs who lived near the Cushites against Jehoram. ¹⁷ They went up against Judah and broke it open. They carried off everything they found in the palace, including Jehoram's sons and wives, until he had no sons left except for Ahaziah, his youngest son. ¹⁸ After all this, the LORD afflicted his bowels with an illness that had no cure. ¹⁹ It went on day after day, until at the end of two *years* his bowels came out, and he died in agony. His people did not make a bonfire in his honorᵇ like they did for his ancestors. ²⁰ He was thirty-two years old when he became king, and he reigned for eight years in Jerusalem. He departed, to no one's regret, and they buried him in the City of David, though not in the tombs of the kings.

2 Chronicles 22

Ahaziah's Evil Reign over Judah

¹ The inhabitants of Jerusalem made Ahaziah, the youngest son *of Jehoram*, king in his place—for all the older sons had been killed by the Arab raiders who had attacked the camp. So Ahaziah son of Jehoram reigned as king over Judah.

² Ahaziah was twenty-twoᶜ years old when he became king, and he reigned one year in Jerusalem. His mother's name was Athaliah, a granddaughter of Omri. ³ He also walked in the ways of Ahab's family, because his mother encouraged him to act wickedly. ⁴ He did evil in the eyes of the LORD like Ahab's family, for they were his

---

a See "Life of Elijah" map and table at 1 Kings 17.

b Literally, "for him."

c From the Septuagint and 2 Kings 8:26; Masoretic text: "forty-two."

advisers after the death of his father, to his undoing. [5] Following their advice, he even went with Joram son of Ahab, King of *Northern* Israel, to fight against Hazael king of Aram at Ramoth Gilead, where the Arameans wounded Joram. [6] So he returned to Jezreel to recover from the wounds he received at Ramah, fighting against Hazael king of Aram. Ahaziah[a] son of Jehoram, king of Judah, went down to visit Joram son of Ahab in Jezreel, because he had been wounded.

[7] When Ahaziah went to visit Joram, his downfall came from God. When he arrived, he went out with Joram to *meet* Jehu son of Nimshi, whom the Lord had anointed to destroy the family of Ahab. [8] While Jehu was executing judgment on the family of Ahab, he found the princes of Judah and the sons of Ahaziah's relatives, who were attending him, and he killed them. [9] Then Jehu hunted Ahaziah, and they caught him while he was hiding in Samaria. He was brought to Jehu and executed. They buried him, because they said, "He was the grandson of Jehoshaphat, who sought the Lord with all his heart." So there was no one in the family of Ahaziah who was able to retain the kingdom.

Athaliah's Rebellion and Downfall

[10] When Athaliah mother of Ahaziah saw that her son was dead, she moved to exterminate every royal child of the house of Judah. [11] But Jehosheba, a daughter of the king, took Joash son of Ahaziah and rescued him from among the king's sons who were being murdered. And she put him and his nurse in a bedroom. Thus Jehosheba (the daughter of King Jehoram and the wife of the priest Jehoiada), because she was Ahaziah's sister, hid the boy from Athaliah so she could not murder him. [12] He remained *hidden* with them in the temple of God for six years while Athaliah ruled the land.

23 *2 Chronicles*

[1] Jehoiada *the priest* gathered his courage in the seventh year. He made a covenant with the captains of hundreds:

Azariah son of Jeroham	Azariah son of Obed
Ishmael son of Jehohanan	Maaseiah son of Adaiah
	Elishaphat son of Zicri

[2] They circulated throughout Judah and gathered the Levites from all the towns of Judah and the family heads from all Israel, and they came to Jerusalem. [3] And the whole assembly made a covenant with the king at the temple of God. Jehoiada instructed them, "Look, the king's son will reign just as the Lord promised concerning the descendants of David.

[4] This is what you are to do:

Priests and Levites:

One third come in on the Sabbath to be gatekeepers,

[5] one third *remain* at the palace, and

one third *remain* at the Foundation Gate.

---

a   Several ancient witnesses and 2 Kings 8:29; Masoretic text: "Azariah."

All the *other* people:

> *Be* in the courts of the temple of the Lord.

6 "No one is to enter the temple of the Lord except the priests and the Levites who assist them. They may enter because they are holy.

> But all the people keep the charge of the Lord!

7 The Levites are to surround the king (*i.e., Joash*), every man with his weapon in his hand. Anyone who enters the temple must be killed. Stay with the king wherever he is."*a*

8 The Levites and all Judah did everything Jehoiada the priest commanded. Each one took his men who were to come on duty on the Sabbath and those who were going off duty on the Sabbath to Jehoiada the priest, for he had not dismissed any of the divisions. 9 Jehoiada the priest equipped the captains of hundreds with the spears and large and small shields that had belonged to David and were in the temple of God. 10 He stationed all the people, each with his weapon in his hand, from the right side of the temple to the left side, near the altar and the temple, surrounding the *future* king. 11 Then they brought out *Joash*, the son of King *Ahaziah,* placed the crown on him *and handed him* the laws the testimony *of Moses*. They proclaimed him king. Jehoiada and his sons anointed him and said, "*Long* live the king!"

12 When Athaliah heard the sound of people running and praising the king, she went out to the people at the temple of the Lord. 13 She looked and was surprised to see the king was standing by his pillar at the entrance. The commanders and trumpeters were beside the king, and all the people of the land were rejoicing and sounding trumpets, and the musicians were leading the praises with their instruments. Then Athaliah tore her clothes and shouted, "Treason! Treason!"

14 Jehoiada the priest brought out the captains of hundreds who were appointed over the troops and said to them, "Take her out between the ranks and kill with the sword anyone who follows her," for the priest had said, "Do not put her to death in the temple of the Lord." 15 So they seized her and took her to the gate where the horses entered the palace, and they executed her there.

16 Jehoiada made a covenant between himself, all the people, and the king, that they would be the people of the Lord. 17 Then all the people went to the temple of Baal and pulled it down, breaking its altars and idols into pieces. And they killed Mattan the priest of Baal in front of the altars. 18 Jehoiada placed the oversight of the temple of the Lord in the hands of the Levitical priests, whom David had assigned to the temple of the Lord—to offer burnt offerings to the Lord as written in the Law of Moses, with joyful singing as David had instructed. 19 The gatekeepers were stationed at the gates of the temple of the Lord so that no one unclean in any way could enter. 20 Jehoiada took the captains of hundreds, the leading men, the rulers of the people, and all the people of the land and brought the king down from the temple of the Lord. They entered the palace by way of the Upper Gate and set the king on the royal throne. 21 All the people of the land rejoiced, and the city was quiet, because Athaliah had been executed with the sword.

---

a   Literally, "when he comes in and when he goes out."

Joash's Reign over Judah

[1] Joash was seven years old when he became king, and he reigned for forty years in Jerusalem. His mother's name was Zibiah from Beersheba. [2] Joash did what was right in the eyes of the LORD all the days of Jehoiada the priest. [3] Jehoiada procured two wives for him, and he had sons and daughters.

Joash's Reforms

[4] Some time later it was on Joash's heart to refurbish the temple of the LORD. [5] He assembled the priests and Levites and said to them, "Go out to the cities of Judah and collect the *yearly tax* in silver from all Israel to refurbish the temple of the LORD. Do it at once." But the Levites delayed.

[6] So the king called Jehoiada the chief *priest* and said, "Why haven't you required the Levites to bring in from Judah and Jerusalem the tax imposed by Moses the servant of the LORD on the assembly of Israel for *the service of* the meeting tent?"[a] [7] (The sons of that evil woman Athaliah had broken into the temple of God and had even used the sacred things in the temple of the LORD for the *worship of* Baal.) [8] Then the king gave an order, and they built a chest and set it outside the gate of the temple of the LORD. [9] They made a proclamation throughout Judah and Jerusalem to bring to the LORD the tax *imposed by* Moses the servant of GOD on Israel in the wilderness.

[10] All the officers and all the people rejoiced. They brought *their tax payments* and dropped them into the chest until it was full. [11] Whenever the chest was carried in[b] to the royal officer by the Levites and they saw that there was a large amount of money, the king's recorder and the chief priest's officer would come, empty the chest, and return it to its place. They did this daily, collecting a large amount of money. [12] The king and Jehoiada gave it to those who were laboring[c] in the temple of the LORD— masons and carpenters who had been hired to refurbish the temple of the LORD, and iron and bronze workers who were reinforcing it. [13] The workmen did the work, and the repairs progressed due to the work of their hands. They rebuilt the temple of God according to its specifications and reinforced it. [14] And when they finished, they brought the remainder of the money to the king and Jehoiada, and he used it to make articles for the temple of the LORD: articles for ministry, for burnt offerings, for dishes, and *other* objects of gold and silver. They were continually offering burnt offerings in the temple of the LORD all the days of Jehoiada.

Joash Turns from God, Is Defeated, and Dies

[15] Jehoiada grew old and full of days, and he died. He was 130 years old when he died. [16] They buried him with the kings in the City of David, because he had done much good in Israel and for the house of his God.

---

a   Literally, "tent of the testimony."
b   Literally, "brought in by the hand of."
c   Literally, "those who did the work of service."

[17] The officials of Judah came and bowed down to the king after Jehoiada died. Then the king listened to them. [18] They abandoned the temple of the LORD, the God of their ancestors, and served*a* the Asherah poles and the idols. So, because of their guilt, the wrath *of the Lord* came upon Judah and Jerusalem. [19] Yet he sent them prophets to turn them back to the LORD and admonish them, but they did not listen.

[20] Then the Spirit of God clothed Zechariah the son of Jehoiada the priest. He stood before the people and said to them, "God says this: 'Why are you transgressing the commands of the LORD? You will not prosper. Because you have abandoned the LORD, he has abandoned you.'" [21] But they conspired against him, and at the order of the king, they stoned him in the courtyard of the temple of the LORD. [22] King Joash did not remember the loyal love that Zechariah's father Jehoiada showed him, and he killed his son.

As Zechariah was dying, he said, "May the LORD see this and seek *vengeance!*"

[23] At the turn of the year (*i.e., springtime*), the Aramean army went up against Joash and invaded Judah and Jerusalem. They slaughtered all the leaders of the people and sent all the plunder to the king in Damascus. [24] Although the Aramean army came with few men, the LORD delivered a much larger army into their hand. For Judah had forsaken the LORD, the God of their ancestors, so they executed *God's* judgment on Joash. [25] When the Arameans withdrew from him (for they had left him severely wounded), his servants plotted against him because *he had spilled* the blood of the son of Jehoiada the priest. They murdered Joash on his bed. So he died, and they buried him in the City of David, but not among the tombs of the kings. [26] Those who had plotted against him were Zabad son of the Ammonite woman Shimeath and Jehozabad son of the Moabite woman Shimrith.

[27] *The account of* his sons, the many oracles about him, and the rebuilding of the temple of God—take a look, they're recorded in the commentary on*b* the Book of the Kings. His son Amaziah reigned in his place.

2 Chronicles **25**

Amaziah's Reign over Judah

[1] Amaziah was twenty-five years old when he became king, and he reigned for twenty-nine years in Jerusalem. His mother's name was Jehoaddin of Jerusalem. [2] He did what was right in the eyes of the LORD, but not wholeheartedly. [3] When he had a firm hold on the kingdom, he executed the servants who had killed his father the king. [4] But he did not execute their sons, as it is written in the Law in the Book of Moses (where the LORD commanded, "Parents shall not be put to death because of *the sins of* their children, nor children be put to death because of *the sins of* their parents. Each one shall be put to death for their own sin"*c*).

[5] Then Amaziah assembled *the men of* Judah, and according to family, appointed over them commanders of thousands and captains of hundreds. *He did this* throughout Judah and Benjamin, mustering those from twenty years old and up. They numbered

---

a   Or "worshiped."
b   Or "the treatise of."
c   See Deuteronomy 24:16.

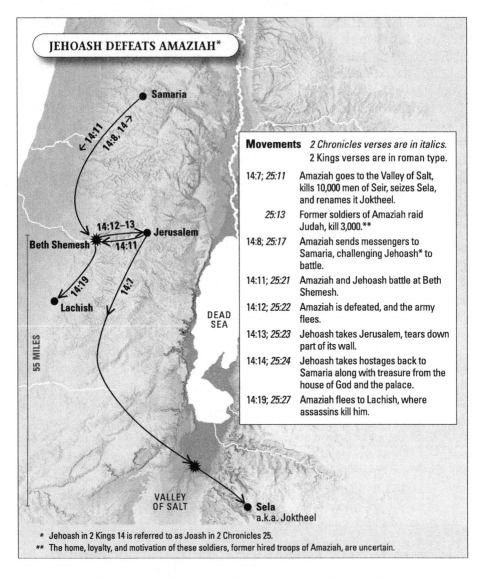

JEHOASH DEFEATS AMAZIAH*

Samaria

14:11
14:8, 14

14:12–13   Jerusalem
Beth Shemesh   14:11

14:19   14:7

Lachish   DEAD
                             SEA
55 MILES

VALLEY
OF SALT   Sela
                     a.k.a. Joktheel

Movements   *2 Chronicles verses are in italics.*
                2 Kings verses are in roman type.

14:7; *25:11*   Amaziah goes to the Valley of Salt, kills 10,000 men of Seir, seizes Sela, and renames it Joktheel.

25:13   Former soldiers of Amaziah raid Judah, kill 3,000.**

14:8; *25:17*   Amaziah sends messengers to Samaria, challenging Jehoash* to battle.

14:11; *25:21* Amaziah and Jehoash battle at Beth Shemesh.

14:12; *25:22* Amaziah is defeated, and the army flees.

14:13; *25:23* Jehoash takes Jerusalem, tears down part of its wall.

14:14; *25:24* Jehoash takes hostages back to Samaria along with treasure from the house of God and the palace.

14:19; *25:27* Amaziah flees to Lachish, where assassins kill him.

* Jehoash in 2 Kings 14 is referred to as Joash in 2 Chronicles 25.
** The home, loyalty, and motivation of these soldiers, former hired troops of Amaziah, are uncertain.

three hundred thousand choice *troops able* to go to war, *able* to handle a spear and large shield. ⁶ Then he hired one hundred thousand warriors from *Ephraim in Northern* Israel for seventy-five hundred pounds*ᵃ* of silver.

⁷ But a man of God came to the king and said, "O king, the *Northern* Israelite mercenaries*ᵇ* should not go up with you, for the Lᴏʀᴅ is not with *Northern* Israel, *not with* any of those Ephraimites! ⁸ Even if you go—go and are courageous in battle—God will throw you down before the enemy, for God has the power to help you or throw you down."

⁹ Amaziah replied to the man of God, "But what shall I do about the seventy-five hundred pounds *of silver* I gave to the *Northern* Israelite mercenaries?"

a   Literally, "100 talents"; and verse 9.
b   Literally, "army"; and verses 9, 10, and 13.

The man of God replied, "The Lord is able to give you much more than that." ¹⁰ So Amaziah dismissed the mercenaries who had come to him from Ephraim—to walk home. They became furious with Judah and returned home in a great rage.

¹¹ But Amaziah gathered his courage and led his army to the Valley of Salt. They struck down ten thousand men of Seir. ¹² The Judahites took ten thousand captives alive and brought them to the edge of the cliff and threw them all down from there, and they were dashed to pieces. ¹³ Meanwhile, the mercenary troops whom Amaziah had discharged, and not taken to war with him, raided the cities of Judah from Samaria to Beth Horon. They killed three thousand people and carried away a large amount of plunder.

¹⁴ After Amaziah returned from destroying the Edomites, he brought the idols of the people of Seir with him and set them up to be his gods. He bowed down and burned incense before them. ¹⁵ The anger of the Lord was aroused against Amaziah, and he sent a prophet to him, who said to him, "Why are you consorting with this people's gods, who could not save their people from your hand?"

¹⁶ While he was still speaking, the king replied, "Have we appointed you an adviser to the king? Stop! Why be put to death?"

So the prophet stopped but said, "I know that God has decided to destroy you, because you have done this and not listened to my counsel."

¹⁷ Amaziah king of Judah consulted *his advisors* and sent messengers to Joash*ᵃ* son of Jehoahaz, son of Jehu, king of *Northern* Israel, saying, "Come, let's look one another in the face *in battle.*"

¹⁸ Joash king of *Northern* Israel sent *messengers* to Amaziah king of Judah to reply, "A thornbush in Lebanon sent word to a cedar in Lebanon, demanding, 'Give your daughter to my son as a wife.' But then a wild beast in Lebanon came by and trampled the thornbush. ¹⁹ You said, 'Look, I have beaten Edom!' You are now arrogant and proud. Now stay home! Why stir up trouble and fall, you and Judah with you?"

²⁰ But Amaziah did not listen, because this was from God, in order to put them in the hand of their enemies, because they had sought the gods of Edom. ²¹ Then Joash king of *Northern* Israel went up, and he and Amaziah king of Judah faced one another *in battle* at Beth Shemesh (which is in Judah). ²² Judah was defeated by *Northern* Israel, and everyone fled to his own home.*ᵇ* ²³ Then Joash king of *Northern* Israel captured Amaziah king of Judah, son of Joash, son of Ahaziah,*ᶜ* at Beth Shemesh. He brought him to Jerusalem and tore down its wall from the Gate of Ephraim to the Corner Gate, *a distance of* two hundred yards.*ᵈ* ²⁴ He *took* all the gold, silver, and articles that were found in the temple of God with *the gatekeeper* Obed-Edom as well as the treasures of the palace, and *he took* hostages. Then he returned to Samaria.

²⁵ Amaziah son of Joash, king of Judah, lived for fifteen years after the death of Joash son of Jehoahaz, king of *Northern* Israel. ²⁶ The rest of the matters regarding

a   Joash is referred to as Jehoash in 2 Kings 14.
b   Literally, "his own tent."
c   Literally, "Jehoahaz," an alternate spelling of "Ahaziah."
d   Literally, "400 cubits."

Amaziah, from beginning to end—take a look, they're recorded in the book Kings of Judah and Israel.

²⁷ *The people of Judah* conspired against him in Jerusalem at the time he turned away from following the Lord. So *after the defeat by Joash,* he fled to Lachish, but they sent *assassins* to Lachish after him, and they killed him there. ²⁸ They brought his *body* on horses and buried him with his ancestors in the city of Judah.

26 *2 Chronicles*

Uzziah's Reign over Judah

¹ All the people of Judah took Uzziah, who was sixteen years old, and made him king in his father Amaziah's place. ² It was he who rebuilt Elath and restored it to Judah after Amaziah lay down with his ancestors. ³ Uzziah was sixteen years old when he became king, and he reigned for fifty-two years in Jerusalem. His mother's name was Jecoliah from Jerusalem. ⁴ He did what was right in the eyes of the Lord, just as his father Amaziah had done. ⁵ He sought God in the days of Zechariah (who instructed him in the fear of God[a]). And as long as he sought the Lord, God made him prosper.

⁶ He went out to fight the Philistines and broke through the wall of Gath, the wall of Jabneh, and the wall of Ashdod. Then he rebuilt towns near Ashdod and *elsewhere* among the Philistines. ⁷ God helped him against the Philistines and against the Arabs who were living in Gur Baal, and against the Meunites. ⁸ The Ammonites paid Uzziah tribute. His fame spread as far as the border of Egypt, for he had become very strong.

⁹ Uzziah built towers in Jerusalem at the Corner Gate, the Valley Gate, and at the corner buttress and fortified them. ¹⁰ He built watchtowers in the wilderness and dug many cisterns, because he had large herds in *both* the foothills and the plains. *He also had* farmers and vinedressers in the hill country and fertile fields, for he loved the soil.

¹¹ Uzziah had an army fit for war, ready to go out by divisions according to their assignments,[b] as prepared by Jeiel the secretary and Maaseiah the officer, under the direction of Hananiah, one of the royal officials. ¹² The total number of the family leaders over the mighty army was 2,600. ¹³ Under their command was a force of 307,500 elite troops who could wage war with great power, who helped the king against his enemies. ¹⁴ Uzziah equipped the whole army with small shields, spears, helmets, coats of armor, bows and arrows, and rock slings. ¹⁵ In Jerusalem he made *war* machines for use on the towers and the buttressed corners, invented by skillful men, for shooting arrows and large stones. His reputation went out far and wide, because he was miraculously helped until he became powerful.

¹⁶ But when he became powerful, his heart became proud, leading to his downfall. He rebelled against the Lord his God by entering the temple of the Lord to burn

---

a From many Hebrew manuscripts and other ancient witnesses; Masoretic text: "in the visions of God" or, more literally, "in the seeing of God."

b Literally, "their muster number."

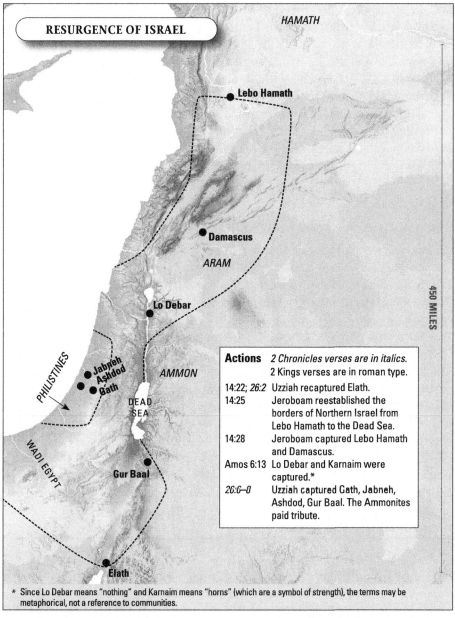

RESURGENCE OF ISRAEL

HAMATH

Lebo Hamath

Damascus

ARAM

Lo Debar

450 MILES

PHILISTINES

Jabneh
Ashdod
Gath

AMMON

DEAD
SEA

WADI EGYPT

Gur Baal

Actions	2 Chronicles verses are in italics.
	2 Kings verses are in roman type.
14:22; *26:2*	Uzziah recaptured Elath.
14:25	Jeroboam reestablished the borders of Northern Israel from Lebo Hamath to the Dead Sea.
14:28	Jeroboam captured Lebo Hamath and Damascus.
Amos 6:13	Lo Debar and Karnaim were captured.*
26:6–0	Uzziah captured Gath, Jabneh, Ashdod, Gur Baal. The Ammonites paid tribute.

Elath

* Since Lo Debar means "nothing" and Karnaim means "horns" (which are a symbol of strength), the terms may be metaphorical, not a reference to communities.

incense at the altar of incense. [17] Azariah the priest went in after him with eighty other courageous priests of the LORD. [18] They stood opposite King Uzziah and said to him, "It is not *right* for you, Uzziah, to burn incense to the LORD, for this *right* belongs to the priests, the descendants of Aaron, who have been set apart to burn incense. Leave the sanctuary, for you have transgressed and will have no honor *for this* from the LORD our God."

[19] Uzziah, who had a censer in his hand for burning incense, was enraged. While he was raging at the priests, leprosy appeared on his forehead in the sight of the priests who were beside the altar of incense in the temple of the LORD. [20] Azariah

the high priest and all the priests turned to him—and there he was—with a leprous forehead! So they hurried him out of there, and indeed he rushed to leave, for the LORD had struck him.

²¹ King Uzziah was a leper until he died. He lived in an separate house^a because of his leprosy, excluded from the temple of the LORD. His son Jotham was over the palace and governed the people of the land.

²² The rest of the matters regarding Uzziah, from beginning to end, were recorded by the prophet Isaiah son of Amoz. ²³ Uzziah lay down with his ancestors, and they buried him with his ancestors in the cemetery that belonged to the kings, for they said, "He was a leper." His son Jotham reigned in his place.

27 2 Chronicles

Jotham's Righteous Reign over Judah

¹ Jotham was twenty-five years old when he became king, and he reigned for sixteen years in Jerusalem. His mother's name was Jerusha daughter of Zadok. ² He did what was right in the eyes of the LORD, like everything that his father Uzziah had done, except he did not enter the temple of the LORD. The people, however, were still acting corruptly.

³ Jotham rebuilt the Upper Gate of the temple of the LORD and reconstructed the wall of Ophel. ⁴ He built cities in the hill country of Judah and fortified outposts and watchtowers in the forests. ⁵ Jotham fought against the Ammonite king and prevailed against him. That year the Ammonites brought him 7,500 pounds of silver, 65,000 bushels of wheat, and 65,000 bushels^b of barley. They also brought him this much in the second and third years. ⁶ Jotham became powerful because he conducted his ways before the LORD his God.

⁷ The rest of the acts of Jotham, including all his wars and other activities^c—take a look, they're recorded in the book Kings of Israel and Judah. ⁸ Jotham was twenty-five years old when he became king, and he ruled for sixteen years in Jerusalem. ⁹ He lay down with his ancestors, and they buried him in the City of David. His son Ahaz ruled in his place.

28 2 Chronicles

Ahaz' Reign over Judah

¹ Ahaz was twenty years old when he became king, and he reigned for sixteen years in Jerusalem. He did not do what was right in the eyes of the LORD, as his ancestor David *had done.* ² He walked in the ways of the kings of *Northern* Israel and even made molten images for *the worship of* Baal. ³ He burned incense in the Valley of Ben-Hinnom and burned his children in the fire according to the abominable practices of the nations that the LORD had driven out before the Israelites. ⁴ He

---

a   Literally, "a free house."
b   Literally, "100 talents," "10,000 kors," "10,000 kors."
c   Literally, "and his ways."

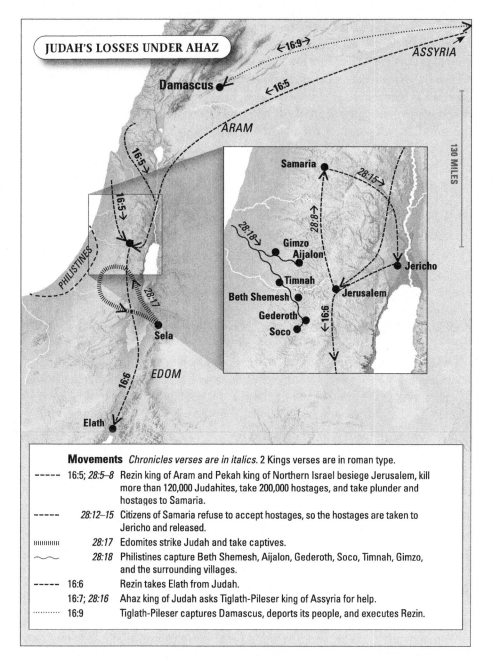

JUDAH'S LOSSES UNDER AHAZ

Movements *Chronicles verses are in italics.* 2 Kings verses are in roman type.

-----	16:5; *28:5–8*	Rezin king of Aram and Pekah king of Northern Israel besiege Jerusalem, kill more than 120,000 Judahites, take 200,000 hostages, and take plunder and hostages to Samaria.
-----	*28:12–15*	Citizens of Samaria refuse to accept hostages, so the hostages are taken to Jericho and released.
ⅢⅢⅢⅢⅢ	*28:17*	Edomites strike Judah and take captives.
~	*28:18*	Philistines capture Beth Shemesh, Aijalon, Gederoth, Soco, Timnah, Gimzo, and the surrounding villages.
-----	16:6	Rezin takes Elath from Judah.
	16:7; *28:16*	Ahaz king of Judah asks Tiglath-Pileser king of Assyria for help.
··········	16:9	Tiglath-Pileser captures Damascus, deports its people, and executes Rezin.

offered sacrifices and burned incense at the high-place shrines, on *other* hilltops, and even beneath every green tree.

⁵ Therefore the LORD his God put him into the hand of the king of Aram, who defeated him and took a huge number of captives from him, taking them to Damascus. He was also put into the hand of the king of *Northern* Israel, who defeated him with a great slaughter. ⁶ Pekah son of Remaliah, king of *Northern* Israel, slew 120,000 in Judah in one day, all of them courageous men, because they

abandoned the Lord, the God of their ancestors. [7] Zicri, a warrior from Ephraim, slew Maaseiah the king's son, Azrikam the leader of the palace *guard,* and Elkanah the second to the king. [8] The *Northern* Israelite army captured two hundred thousand related *Judahites* (women and children) and also a large amount of plunder, which they took to Samaria.

[9] But a prophet of the Lord whose name was Oded was there. He went out before the army as it was returning to Samaria and said to them,

"Look! Because the Lord, the God of your ancestors, was angry with Judah, he put them into your hand. But you have slaughtered them in a rage that has reached to heaven! [10] And now you propose to make the men and women of Judah and Jerusalem your slaves! Aren't you also guilty before the Lord your God? [11] Now listen to me: Return these captives you have taken from your relatives, for the Lord's anger is burning against you."

[12] Then some of the family heads of Ephraim—Azariah son of Jehohanan, Berekiah son of Meshillemoth, Jehizkiah son of Shallum, and Amasa son of Hadlai—stood up against those troops who were returning from the battle. [13] They told them, "Don't bring those captives here! Aren't we guilty before the Lord? You are proposing to add to our sins and our guilt! Our guilt is *already* great, and the anger of the Lord is burning against *Northern* Israel!"

[14] Then the army left the captives and the plunder before the officers and the entire assembly. [15] The men designated by name took the captives and clothed those who were naked, dressing them from the plunder. And they gave them clothes, sandals, food and drink, and healing balm. They put all the weak on donkeys and took everyone back to Jericho, the City of Palms, to their relatives. Then they returned to Samaria.

[16] At that time King Ahaz sent messengers to the kings of Assyria to help him, [17] because the Edomites had invaded Judah and taken captives. [18] And the Philistines had raided towns in the foothills and the Negev of Judah, capturing Beth Shemesh, Aijalon, Gederoth, Soco with its villages, Timnah with its villages, and Gimzo with its villages, and they settled there. [19] For the Lord had humbled Judah because of Ahaz king of *Judean* Israel (because Ahaz had allowed libertinism[a] in Judah, and because he was unfaithful to the Lord). [20] So Tiglath-Pileser king of Assyria came to him, but troubled him rather than strengthening him. [21] Ahaz took a portion *of treasure* from the temple of the Lord and the palace and gave it to the king of Assyria, but it did not help him.

[22] In the time of his distress, King Ahaz became even more unfaithful to the Lord. That was King Ahaz— [23] he sacrificed to the gods of Damascus, *the gods of* those who had defeated him, thinking, "Because the gods of the kings of Aram helped them, I will sacrifice to them so that they will help me." But they became his downfall and that of all Israel. [24] Ahaz gathered the utensils from the temple of God and cut them to pieces—articles of the house of God! He shut the doors of the temple of the Lord and built altars for himself on every corner in Jerusalem. [25] In every single city

---

a   "Libertinism": a lifestyle of self-indulgence and lack of restraint, especially moral restraint.

in Judah he constructed high-place shrines for burning incense to other gods. So he provoked the LORD, the God of his ancestors.

²⁶ The rest of his acts and all his ways, from beginning to end—take a look, they're recorded in the book Kings of Judah and Israel. ²⁷ Ahaz lay down with his ancestors, and they buried him in the City of David,ᵃ but not in the tombs of the kings of Israel. His son Hezekiah reigned in his place.

2 Chronicles **29**

Hezekiah's Righteous Reign over Judah

¹ Hezekiah was twenty-five years old when he became king, and he reigned for twenty-nine years in Jerusalem. His mother's name was Abijah daughter of Zechariah. ² He did what was right in the eyes of the LORD, like everything that his ancestor David had done.

Temple Rededication

³ In the first month of the first year of his reign, he opened the doors of the temple of the LORD and repaired them. ⁴ He brought in the priests and the Levites and gathered them in the square on the east side. ⁵ He said to them, "Listen to me, Levites! Now consecrate yourselves and then reconsecrate the temple of the LORD, the God of your ancestors. Remove anything unclean from the sanctuary. ⁶ Our ancestors were unfaithful and did evil in the eyes of the LORD our God. They abandoned him, turned their faces away from the tabernacle of the LORD, and turned their backs on him. ⁷ They also shut the doors of the *temple* porch and put out the lamps. They did not burn incense nor offer burnt offerings in the sanctuary to the God of Israel. ⁸ Therefore the wrath of the LORD came upon Judah and Jerusalem, and he made them an object of terror, horror, and scorn, just as you are seeing with your own eyes. ⁹ Look, our ancestors fell by the sword. Our sons, daughters, and wives are in captivity because of this. ¹⁰ Now it is on my heart to make a covenant with the LORD, the God of Israel, so that he will turn his burning anger from us. ¹¹ Now, my sons, do not be negligent, because the LORD has chosen you to stand before him to minister; to serve and burn incense." ¹² These Levites rose up *to serve*:

Mahath son of Amasai and Joel son of Azariah (Kohathites)
Kish son of Abdi and Azariah son of Jehallelel (Merarites)
Joah son of Zimmah and Eden son of Joah (Gershonites)
¹³ Shimri and Jeiel (descendants of Elizaphan)
Zechariah and Mattaniah (descendants of Asaph)
¹⁴ Jehiel and Shimei (descendants of Heman)
Shemaiah and Uzziel (descendants of Jeduthun)

¹⁵ They gathered their relatives, consecrated themselves, and entered the temple of the LORD to cleanse it, according to the king's command and the word of the LORD. ¹⁶ The priests went into the inner part of the temple of the LORD to cleanse it. They brought every unclean thing they found in the temple of the LORD out to the

---

a   From the Septuagint; Masoretic text: "city of Jerusalem."

courtyard of the temple. The Levites received those things and took them to *burn in* the Kidron Valley. [17] They began the consecration *in early spring,* on the first day of the first month, and they reached the porch of the Lord on the eighth day of the month. Then they consecrated the temple of the Lord for eight *more* days, finishing on the sixteenth day of the first month.

[18] Then they went in to King Hezekiah and said, "We have cleansed the entire temple of the Lord, the altar of burnt offering and all its utensils, the table of the bread of the Presence and all its utensils—[19] all the articles that King Ahaz discarded during his reign and his faithlessness. We have prepared and consecrated them. They're there, in front of the altar of the Lord!"

[20] King Hezekiah got up early *the next day,* gathered the leaders of the city, and went up to the temple of the Lord. [21] They brought seven bulls, seven rams, seven lambs, and seven male goats as a sin offering for the kingdom, for the sanctuary, and for Judah. He ordered the priests, the descendants of Aaron, to offer them on the altar of the Lord. [22] They slaughtered the bulls, and the priests received the blood and sprinkled it on the altar. Then they slaughtered the rams and sprinkled their blood on the altar. Finally, they slaughtered the lambs and sprinkled their blood on the altar.

[23] Then they brought the goats for the sin offering before the king and the assembly. After they laid their hands on them, [24] the priests slaughtered them and with their blood made a sin offering on the altar to atone for *the sins of* all Israel. For the king had ordered the burnt offering and the sin offering for all Israel.

[25] He stationed the Levites in the temple of the Lord with cymbals, harps, and lyres, according to the commandment of David, Gad the king's prophet, and Nathan the prophet, as was commanded by the Lord through his prophets. [26] The Levites stood with the *musical* instruments of David, and the priests stood with trumpets. [27] Then Hezekiah ordered that the burnt offering be brought to the altar. And the song of the Lord began, accompanied by the trumpets and the instruments of King David, when the offering began. [28] All the assembly were worshiping, the music was playing, and the trumpets were blowing all together until the offering was finished. [29] At the conclusion of the offerings, the king and all who were with him bowed down and worshiped. [30] Then King Hezekiah and the officials ordered the Levites to sing praises to the Lord with the words of David and Asaph the prophet. So they sang praises with joy, bowed down, and worshiped.

[31] Then Hezekiah said, "Now you have consecrated yourselves to the Lord.[a] Come up and bring sacrifices and thank offerings to the temple of the Lord."

The assembly brought sacrifices and thank offerings, and everyone who was willing *brought* burnt offerings. [32] The number of burnt offerings that the assembly brought was seventy bulls, one hundred rams, and two hundred lambs—all for burnt offerings to the Lord. [33] The consecrated things were six hundred bulls and three thousand sheep and goats. [34] But the priests were too few and were not able to skin all the burnt offerings, so their brothers the Levites helped[b] them until the

---

a Literally, "Now you have filled your hands toward the Lord."
b Literally, "strengthened."

task was complete and until *other* priests had consecrated themselves *in sufficient numbers*. The Levites were more conscientious^a about consecrating themselves than the priests. ³⁵ There were burnt offerings galore, and fat from the peace offerings, and drink offerings that accompanied the burnt offerings. So the service of the temple of the LORD was reestablished. ³⁶ And Hezekiah and all the people rejoiced because of what God had established for the people, because the consecration^b had been brought about so quickly.

2 Chronicles **30**

Passover Restoration

¹ Hezekiah sent messengers to all *Northern* Israel and Judah, and he also wrote letters to *the tribes of* Ephraim and Manasseh, to come to the temple of the LORD in Jerusalem to celebrate the Passover to the LORD, the God of Israel. ² The king, the leaders, and the entire assembly in Jerusalem decided to celebrate the Passover in the second month, ³ because they were unable to celebrate it at the *proper time*^c—for the priests were not consecrated in sufficient number, and the people were not gathered in Jerusalem. ⁴ This seemed right in the eyes of the king and the whole assembly. ⁵ They decided to make a proclamation^d throughout Israel, from Beersheba to Dan, *that people were* to come and celebrate the Passover to the LORD God of Israel in Jerusalem, because for many *years* they had not done *it* according to what was written. ⁶ The messengers went to all *Northern* Israel and Judah, as directed by the command of the king, with letters from the hand of the king and his officials, which read:

> ### Proclamation of King Hezekiah
>
> O people of Israel,
>   Return to the LORD, the God of Abraham, Isaac, and Israel!
>   Then he will return to the survivors,
>   the remnant of you who have escaped from the hand of
>   the kings of Assyria.
> ⁷ Do not be like your ancestors or your relatives
>   who were unfaithful to the LORD, the God of their ancestors,
>   such that he made them an object of horror like you see.
> ⁸ Do not now stiffen your necks like your ancestors, but
>   submit yourself to the LORD;
>   come to his sanctuary, which he consecrated forever.
>   Serve^e the LORD your God.

---

a   Literally, "upright in heart."
b   Literally, "the thing."
c   "The proper time": the fourteenth day of the first month. (See Exodus 12:1–11.)
d   Literally, "a noise."
e   Or "worship."

He will turn his fierce anger from you.
⁹ For if you turn to the Lord,
    your fellow Israelites and your children *will find* compassion
        before those who took them captive, and
    they will return to this land.
For the Lord your God is gracious and compassionate.
He will not turn his face from you if you return to him.

¹⁰ The messengers passed from town to town in the lands of Ephraim and Manasseh, as far as Zebulun. But the inhabitants*ᵃ* laughed at them and ridiculed them. ¹¹ Nevertheless, *some* men from Asher, Manasseh, and Zebulun humbled themselves and went to Jerusalem. ¹² The hand of God was also on Judah, giving them one heart—to carry out the commands of the king and the leaders according to the word of the Lord.

¹³ In the spring,*ᵇ* a vast crowd, a massive assembly, gathered themselves to observe the Feast of Unleavened Bread. ¹⁴ They set to work and removed all the *foreign* altars and incense altars in Jerusalem and threw them into the Kidron Valley. ¹⁵ Then they slaughtered the Passover *lambs* on the fourteenth day of the second month. The priests and Levites were ashamed *of themselves*, so they consecrated themselves. Then they brought their burnt offerings to the temple of the Lord. ¹⁶ They stood at their stations according to the ordinance in the Law of Moses the man of God. The priests sprinkled the blood *that they received* from the hand of the Levites. ¹⁷ Since many in the assembly had not consecrated themselves, the Levites were in charge of slaughtering the Passover *lambs* for all who were unclean, in order to consecrate *the lambs* to the Lord. ¹⁸ A large number of the people, many from Ephraim, Manasseh, Issachar, and Zebulun, had not purified themselves, yet they ate the Passover *anyway,* contrary to the written *instructions.* This was because Hezekiah had prayed for them, saying, "May the good Lord pardon ¹⁹ everyone whose heart is set on seeking God, the Lord, the God of their ancestors, although not according to the cleanliness *rules* of the sanctuary." ²⁰ The Lord listened to Hezekiah and healed the people.

²¹ The Israelites who were present*ᶜ* in Jerusalem celebrated the Feast of Unleavened Bread for seven days with great joy. And the Levites and priests were praising the Lord day after day with loud instruments *dedicated* to the Lord. ²² Hezekiah spoke encouragingly to all the Levites who had a good understanding of the Lord. So they ate for the appointed seven days, sacrificing peace offerings and giving thanks to the Lord, the God of their ancestors.

²³ The whole assembly decided to celebrate for seven more days. They celebrated for seven *more* days with joy, ²⁴ for Hezekiah king of Judah had provided the assembly with one thousand bulls and seven thousand sheep and goats; and the leaders provided one thousand bulls and ten thousand sheep and goats to the

---

a   Literally, "But they."
b   Literally, "In the second month."
c   Literally, "who were found in."

assembly. And a large number of priests consecrated themselves. ²⁵ The whole assembly of Judah—the priests, the Levites, the assembly who had come from *Northern* Israel, and the foreigners who came from the land of *Northern* Israel and stayed in Judah—rejoiced. ²⁶ So there was great joy in Jerusalem, because there had been nothing like this in Jerusalem since the days of Israel's King Solomon son of David. ²⁷ The priests and Levites got up to bless the people, and their voice was heard. Their prayer entered *God's* holy dwelling place in heaven.

2 Chronicles **31**

Hezekiah's Worship Reforms

¹ After all this was finished, all *the people of* Israel who were present in the cities of Judah went out and shattered the sacred stones, cut down the Asherah poles, and tore down the high-place shrines and altars throughout Judah, Benjamin, Ephraim, and Manasseh until they were *all* destroyed. Then all the Israelites returned *home* to their own possessions and towns.

² Hezekiah stationed the priests and Levites according to their divisions, each according to his service as a priest or a Levite—to offer burnt and peace offerings, to minister, and to give thanks and praise at the gates of the camp of the Lord.

³ As it is written in the Law of the Lord, the king's portion *given* for the burnt offerings for mornings, evenings, Sabbaths, New Moon *Festivals,* and appointed festivals was from his personal property. ⁴ He ordered the people who were inhabitants of Jerusalem to contribute the portion *due* to the priests and Levites so that they could devote themselves to the Law of the Lord.ᵃ ⁵ When this command went out, the Israelites brought an abundance of the firstfruits of their wheat, wine, olive oil, honey, and all that their fields produced—large quantities, the tithe of everything. ⁶ The *Northern* Israelites and Judahites who lived in the towns of Judah even brought a tithe of their cattle, sheep, and goats, and a tithe of the holy things that were dedicated to the Lord their God, *which* they piled in heaps. ⁷ They began piling up the heaps in late spring and finished in early fall.ᵇ ⁸ When Hezekiah and the leaders saw the piles, they blessed the Lord and his people Israel. ⁹ Hezekiah asked the priests and Levites about the piles. ¹⁰ Azariah the high priest, of the family of Zadok, answered, "Since the people began to bring their contributions to the temple of the Lord, we have eaten our fill and had plenty left over, because the Lord has blessed his people. This great quantity is left over!"

¹¹ So Hezekiah ordered *them* to set up storerooms in the temple of the Lord, and they did so. ¹²ᵃ They faithfully brought in the contributions, tithes, and dedicated things.

Temple Staff [31:12b-15]	
Appointed by King Hezekiah [13b]	
Official in charge [12b,13b] of the temple of the Lord	Azariah
Overseeing officer	Conaniah, a Levite
Second *officer*	Shimei, Conaniah's brother
Overseers [13a]	Jehiel, Azaziah, Nahath, Asahel, Jerimoth, Jozabad, Eliel, Ismakiah, Mahath, and Benaiah
Keeper of the East Gate [14]	Kore son of Imnah the Levite. He was in charge of the freewill offerings to God. He also distributed the contributions to the LORD and the consecrated things.

Assistant gatekeepers[a] [15]	Eden	Jeshua	Amariah
	Miniamin	Shemaiah	Shecaniah

The assistants made disbursements[b] to
>their relatives the priests in their towns,
>>according to their divisions, great and small,
>16 without regard for their *place in* genealogical records—
>>all males three years old and up,
>>all who would enter the temple of the LORD for their daily responsibilities,
>>>for their work and service according to their divisions;
17 as well as to
>the priests who were enrolled genealogically according to their families, and
>the Levites twenty years old and up according to their responsibilities and divisions.

18 The genealogical enrollment *included* all their little ones, wives, sons, and daughters of the whole assembly, for they were faithful in consecrating themselves. 19 As for the priests, the descendants of Aaron, *who lived* in the pasturelands around each and every one of their cities, there were men designated by name to distribute portions to every male among the priests and to everyone enrolled in the genealogies of the Levites.

20 Hezekiah did this throughout Judah, doing what was good, right, and faithful before the LORD his God. 21 He sought his God in all the work he began for the service of the temple of the LORD, according to the Law and the commandment. He did *everything* with all his heart, and he prospered.

32 2 Chronicles

Victory over Sennacherib's Invasion

1 After *Hezekiah proved to be* true in these matters, Sennacherib king of Assyria invaded Judah. He besieged the fortified cities and thought to cut them out for his own *empire.* 2 When Hezekiah saw that Sennacherib had come and intended to

---

a Literally, "under his authority."
b Whether the disbursements were monetary, food from sacrifices, or something else is unclear.

make war*a* against Jerusalem, ³ he conferred with his leaders and warriors about plugging the springs of water, which were outside the city, and they helped him. ⁴ A large *number of* people gathered to stop every spring and the stream that flowed through the land. They said, "Why should the kings of Assyria come and find plenty of water?"

⁵ Hezekiah strengthened *the city*. He built up all the broken sections of the wall, raised towers on it, and built *another* wall outside. He reinforced the terraces*b* in the City of David and made large numbers of weapons and shields. ⁶ He put battle commanders over the people and rallied them to himself in the square at the city gate. He encouraged them, saying, ⁷ "Be strong and courageous! Do not be afraid or terrified before the king of Assyria or all the great horde with him, for *he who is* with you is greater than *those who are* with him. ⁸ With him is *only* the arm of flesh, but the Lord our God is with us to help us and fight our battles." And the people relied on the words of King Hezekiah of Judah.

⁹ After this, while he was besieging Lachish with all his army, Sennacherib king of Assyria sent his servants to Jerusalem—to Hezekiah king of Judah and all the Judahites in Jerusalem—saying, ¹⁰ "Sennacherib king of Assyria says this:

'What are you trusting in, that you stay in Jerusalem under siege? ¹¹ Isn't Hezekiah deceiving you so that you will be given over to death by famine and thirst, saying, "The Lord our God will save us from the hand of the king of Assyria"? ¹² Hasn't this Hezekiah removed the high-place shrines and altars and commanded Judah and Jerusalem to bow down and burn sacrifices*c* at only one altar? ¹³ Do you not know what I and my fathers have done to all the peoples of the *other* lands? Were *any of* the nations' gods in *other* lands actually able to rescue their land from my hand? ¹⁴ Who among all the gods of those nations whom my fathers completely destroyed has rescued his people from my hand? Then how will your God save you from my hand? ¹⁵ Now don't let Hezekiah deceive you or mislead you like this. Do not believe him, for no god of any people or kingdom has been able to save his people from my hand or the hand of my fathers. How much less will your God be able to save you from my hand!' "

¹⁶ Sennacherib's servants continued to speak against the Lord God and his servant Hezekiah. ¹⁷ He wrote letters to taunt the Lord God of Israel and to speak against him, saying, "The God of Hezekiah will not save his people from my hand, just like the gods of the peoples of the *other* lands were not able to save their people from my hand." ¹⁸ They called out in a loud voice in Hebrew to the people of Jerusalem on the wall to frighten and discourage them so that they could capture the city. ¹⁹ They spoke against the God of Jerusalem just like they did against the gods of the peoples of the earth—the work of human hands.

²⁰ King Hezekiah and the prophet Isaiah son of Amoz prayed about this and cried out to heaven. ²¹ So the Lord sent an angel who cut down every warrior, leader, and commander in the camp of the king of Assyria. He returned to his land with

---

a   Literally, "come, his face to make war."
b   Literally, "strengthened the *millo*." The meaning of *millo* is uncertain.
c   Or "burn incense."

shame on his face. He went to the temple of his god, where his own offspring cut him down with the sword. ²² So the LORD saved Hezekiah and all the inhabitants of Jerusalem from the hand of Sennacherib king of Assyria and from the hand of all others, and gave them rest on every side. ²³ And many were bringing gifts to the LORD in Jerusalem and choice gifts to King Hezekiah of Judah. From then on he was highly exalted in the eyes of all the nations.

Hezekiah's Last Days and Death

²⁴ In those days Hezekiah became ill to the point of death. He prayed to the LORD, who spoke to him and gave him a sign. ²⁵ But Hezekiah did not respond to the favor shown him, for his heart became proud. So the wrath *of God* came upon him, Judah, and Jerusalem. ²⁶ But Hezekiah humbled himself regarding his proud heart, he and all the inhabitants of Jerusalem with him. So the wrath of the LORD did not come upon them during the days of Hezekiah.

²⁷ Hezekiah had great riches and was highly honored. He built treasuries for himself for silver, gold, precious stones, spices, shields, and all kinds of valuable items. ²⁸ *He also built* storehouses for the harvests of grain, wine, and olive oil, and stables for every kind of cattle, and pens for the flocks. ²⁹ He built cities for himself and acquired huge flocks and herds, for God had given him tremendous wealth.

³⁰ It was Hezekiah who plugged the upper opening of the Gihon Spring and directed the water downward to the west side of the City of David. Hezekiah succeeded in everything he did. ³¹ But regarding the envoys of the rulers of Babylon, who were sent to ask him about the wonder that had occurred in the land, God withdrew from him to test him and know everything that was in his heart.

³² The rest of the matters regarding Hezekiah and his faithful acts—take a look, they're recorded in the oracle of the prophet Isaiah son of Amoz in the book Kings of Judah and Israel. ³³ Hezekiah lay down with his ancestors, and they buried him in the upper *section* of[a] the tombs of the descendants of David. All Judah and the inhabitants of Jerusalem paid him honor at his death. His son Manasseh reigned in his place.

33 *2 Chronicles*

Manasseh's Evil Reign over Judah

¹ Manasseh was twelve years old when he became king. He reigned for fifty-five years in Jerusalem. ² He did evil in the eyes of the LORD, *following* the evil practices of the nations the LORD had driven out before the Israelites. ³ He

> rebuilt the high-place shrines that his father Hezekiah had torn down;
> erected altars for the images of Baal;
> erected Asherah *poles*;
> bowed down to the armies of *the stars in* the sky and served them *all*; and
> ⁴ built altars in the temple of the LORD,
> > *about* which the LORD had said, "In Jerusalem my name will be forever."

---

a   Or "on the slope up to."

⁵ He built altars for the armies of *the stars* in the sky in the two courts of the temple of the Lᴏʀᴅ! ⁶ And he

sacrificed his children by fire in*ᵃ* the Valley of the Son of Hinnom, practicing

| spiritism, | magic, and |
| divination, | necromancy*ᵇ* with many evil spirits. |

He did much evil in the eyes of the Lᴏʀᴅ, provoking his anger. ⁷ He even put the carved image, the idol that he made, in the temple of God—*the temple* of which God said to David and his son Solomon,

"In this house and in Jerusalem, which I have chosen out of all the tribes of Israel, I have put my name forever. ⁸ I will not remove the foot of Israel again from the land where I established their ancestors—provided that they keep doing all that I commanded them; all the instructions, statutes, and regulations *that I declared* by the hand of Moses."

⁹ But Manasseh led astray the *tribe of* Judah and the residents of Jerusalem, such that they did more evil than the nations the Lᴏʀᴅ had exterminated before the Israelites.

Manasseh's Repentance and Death

¹⁰ The Lᴏʀᴅ spoke to Manasseh and his people, but they did not listen. ¹¹ So the Lᴏʀᴅ brought upon them the generals of the army of the king of Assyria. They captured Manasseh among the thickets,*ᶜ* bound him in bronze *chains*, and took him to Babylon. ¹² During the time of his imprisonment,*ᵈ* he softened the face of the Lᴏʀᴅ his God and humbled himself profoundly before the God of his ancestors. ¹³ He prayed to God, and he was moved. He listened to his request and returned Manasseh to his throne in Jerusalem. Then Manasseh knew that the Lᴏʀᴅ is the only God.

¹⁴ After this, he

built the outer wall of the City of David,

west of the Gihon *Spring* in the valley, as far as the entrance to the Fish Gate and around the *hill of* Ophel, making it very high. He also

put army commanders in all the fortified cities of Judah. ¹⁵ He removed the foreign gods and the idol

from the temple of the Lᴏʀᴅ and all the altars, which he had built on the Temple Mount and in Jerusalem, and he threw them out of the city. ¹⁶ He restored the altar of the Lᴏʀᴅ

and sacrificed offerings of fellowship and praise on it.

He commanded the people of Judah to serve the Lᴏʀᴅ, the God of Israel.

¹⁷ Nevertheless, the people continued to sacrifice at the high-place shrines, but only to the Lᴏʀᴅ their God.

¹⁸ The rest of the matters regarding Manasseh,

his prayer to his God,

---

a   Or "sacrificed his children in the fire in." Literally, "passed his children through the fire in."
b   "Necromancy": supposedly communicating with the dead.
c   Or "with hooks."
d   Literally, "of his distress."

the words of the prophets who spoke to him in the name of the Lord,
the God of Israel—take a look, they're in the History of the Kings of Israel.
[19] His prayer, how God was moved by him,
all his sins and trespasses,
the sites where he built *shrines* on the high places, and
the Asherah poles and idols he erected before he humbled himself
—take a look, they're in the writings of the prophets.

[20] Manasseh lay down with his fathers, and they buried him in his house. His son Amon reigned in his place.

Amon's Short, Evil Reign over Judah

[21] Amon was twenty-two years old when he became king, and he reigned for two years in Jerusalem. [22] He did evil in the eyes of the Lord, just like his father Manasseh had done. Amon sacrificed to all the idols that his father Manasseh had made, and he served them. [23] He did not, however, humble himself before the Lord like his father Manasseh humbled himself. Amon sinned even more. [24] His officials conspired against him and murdered him in his palace. [25] But the people of the land struck down all those who had conspired against King Amon and made his son Josiah king in his place.

34 *2 Chronicles*

Josiah's Righteous Reign over Judah

[1] Josiah was eight years old when he became king, and he reigned for thirty-one years in Jerusalem. [2] He did what was right in the eyes of the Lord and walked in the ways of his ancestor David. He did not turn aside to the right or to the left. [3] For in the eighth year of his reign, while he was still a youth, he began to seek the God of his ancestor David.

Restoration of the Temple

In the twelfth year *of his reign* he began to cleanse Judah and Jerusalem of the high-place shrines, Asherah poles, idols, and cast images. [4] They tore down the altars of the Baals in his presence[a] and cut down the incense altars that were above them. They broke into pieces the Asherah poles, idols, and cast images. He pulverized them and scattered the fragments over the graves of those who had sacrificed to them. [5] He also burned the bones of the *pagan* priests on their *own* altars. In this way he cleansed Judah and Jerusalem. [6] *He did likewise* in the towns of Manasseh, Ephraim, Simeon, and as far as Naphtali and their surrounding ruins. [7] He tore down the altars and Asherah poles and beat them into pieces and then pulverized them. And he cut down all the incense altars throughout the land of Israel. *Finally*, he returned to Jerusalem.

---

a   Literally, "before him."

⁸ In the eighteenth year of his reign, when he had purified*ᵃ* the land and the temple, he sent Shaphan son of Azaliah, Maaseiah (governor of the city), and Joah son of Joahaz, the recorder, to repair the temple of the LORD his God. ⁹ They came to Hilkiah the high priest and gave him the money that had been brought to the temple of God, which the Levite doorkeepers had collected from all the remaining people of *Northern* Israel (including Manasseh and Ephraim, and all of Judah, Benjamin, and the residents of Jerusalem). ¹⁰ They put it in the hand of those who were appointed to *supervise* the work on the temple of the LORD. These men paid it to those who did the work of repairing and restoring the temple of the LORD. ¹¹ They then gave it to the carpenters and builders to purchase dressed stone and lumber for joists and beams for the structures that the kings of Judah had allowed to fall to ruin.

¹² The men worked with integrity with these foremen over them to supervise: Jahath and Obadiah, the Levites from the family of Merari, and Zechariah and Meshullam, *the Levites* from the family of Kohath. Other Levites, all who were skilled in playing musical instruments, ¹³ were over the porters and supervised the workers from job to job. *Some of* the Levites were secretaries, officials, and gatekeepers.

Reestablishment of the Law

¹⁴ While they were bringing out the money that had been put into the temple of the LORD, Hilkiah the priest found the book of the Law of the LORD, written down by*ᵇ* Moses. ¹⁵ Hilkiah shouted to Shaphan the scribe, "I have found the book of the Law in the temple of the LORD," and he gave the book to Shaphan.

¹⁶ Shaphan brought the book to the king and reassured*ᶜ* him , saying, "Your servants are doing everything they have been assigned to do. ¹⁷ They have spent the money that was found in the temple of the LORD and delivered it into the hand of the foremen and the workers." ¹⁸ In addition, Shaphan the scribe told the king, "Hilkiah the priest gave me a book," and he read it before the king.

¹⁹ When the king heard the words of the Law, he tore his robes. ²⁰ The king commanded Hilkiah, Ahikam son of Shaphan, Abdon son of Micah, Shaphan the scribe, and Asaiah the king's servant, saying, ²¹ "Go and ask the LORD for me and for those who are left in *Northern* Israel and Judah about the words of this book that was found. The wrath of the LORD that is poured out on us is great, because our ancestors did not keep the word of the LORD, to do according to all that is written in this book."

²² So Hilkiah and the others*ᵈ* went to Huldah the prophetess, the wife of Shallum son of Tokhath, son of Hasrah, keeper of the wardrobe. (She lived in the Second Quarter of Jerusalem.) They told her everything that had happened.*ᵉ* ²³ And she replied,

"The LORD God of Israel says this:

'Tell the man who sent you to me: ²⁴ The LORD says this:

---

a   Or "in order to purify."
b   Literally, "by the hand of."
c   "Literally, "reported further word."
d   Literally, "Hilkiah and whom the king *had sent.*"
e   Literally, "told her this."

Look, I am about to bring disaster on this place and its inhabitants—all the curses written in the book that was read before the king of Judah. [25] Because they have abandoned me and burned incense to other gods, provoking my anger with all that their hands have made, I will pour out my anger on this place, and it will not be quenched.

[26] 'But say this to the king of Judah, who sent you to ask the Lord a question: The Lord God of Israel says this *about* the words you have heard:

[27] Because your heart was soft and you humbled yourself before God when you heard his words about this place and its inhabitants, and you humbled yourself before me, tore your robes, and wept before me, I have indeed heard you,' declares the Lord. [28] 'Look, I will gather you to your ancestors, and you will be buried in[a] your grave in peace. You will not see with your eyes all the disaster that I am about to bring on this place and its inhabitants.'"

And they brought *this* report back to the king.

[29] Then the king sent out messengers and gathered all the elders of Judah and Jerusalem. [30] He went up to the temple of the Lord along with all the people of Judah and the inhabitants of Jerusalem, the priests, the Levites, and all the people, from the least to the greatest. And he read in their hearing all the words of the Book of the Covenant, which had been found in the temple of the Lord. [31] The king stood in his place *of authority* and renewed the covenant[b] before the Lord:

to walk after the Lord,
to keep his commandments, decrees, and statutes
    with all his heart and all his soul, and
to act according to[c] the words of the covenant that were written in this book.

[32] He made everyone who was found in Jerusalem and Benjamin stand *with him.* So the inhabitants of Jerusalem did this according to the covenant of God, the God of their ancestors. [33] Then Josiah removed all the abominable things from all the territories belonging to the Israelites. He required all who were present in Israel to serve the Lord their God. For all the days of his *reign,* they did not turn away from the Lord, the God of their ancestors.

35 *2 Chronicles*

Passover Restored Again

[1] Josiah celebrated the Passover to the Lord in Jerusalem. He slaughtered the Passover lamb on the fourteenth day of the first month.[d] [2] He stationed the priests in their places of service and encouraged them in the service of the temple of the Lord. [3] He told the Levites, who instructed all Israel and who were holy to the Lord,

"Put the holy ark in the temple built by Israel's King Solomon son of David.

---

a   Literally, "gathered to."
b   Literally, "cut the covenant."
c   Literally, "to stand on."
d   About March 15.

It is not to be a burden on your shoulders *any longer.*
Now serve the Lord your God and his people Israel.

4 Prepare *yourselves* by families and divisions,
according to the written instructions of David king of Israel and the
written instructions of his son Solomon.

5 Stand in the Holy Place by family groups of your relatives the *lay* people,*a*
according to the Levite divisions of your family groups.

6 Slaughter the Passover *animals* and
consecrate yourselves.

Make preparations for your relatives to act according to the word of the Lord *given*
through Moses."

Passover Sacrifice Contributions 35:7-9	
Josiah Contributed to the lay people as Passover offerings for all who were present. 7	30,000 sheep and goats from the flock 3,000 cattle All from the king's possession
Royal officials in charge of God's temple 8 contributed willingly to the people, the priests, and the Levites.	2,600 sheep and goats and 300 cattle were given to the priests by Hilkiah, Zechariah, and Jehiel.
Leaders of the Levites 9 Conaniah His brothers: Shemaiah and Nethanel Hashabiah Jeiel Jozabad	5,000 sheep and goats and 500 cattle

10 When the service had been set up, at the command of the king, the priests
stood in their places, and the Levites *stood* according to their divisions. 11 Then
they slaughtered the Passover *animals.* The priests sprinkled the blood that was
handed to them against the altar, and the Levites skinned *the animals.* 12 Then they
set aside the burnt offerings to give them to the lay people by family groups to offer
to the Lord, as it is written in the Book of Moses. *They also did* this with the cattle.
13 They roasted the Passover animals over the fire, according to the ordinance, and
they boiled the holy parts in pots, kettles, and pans and served them quickly to the
people. 14 Afterward they made preparations for themselves and for the priests, the
descendants of Aaron, because they were *busy* sacrificing the burnt offerings and fat
portions *from morning* till night (so the Levites had to prepare for themselves as well
as the priests, the sons of Aaron). 15 The musicians, the descendants of Asaph, were
in their places according to the instructions of David, Asaph, Heman, and Jeduthun
the king's prophet. The gatekeepers were at all the gates. They did not have to leave
their *places of* service, because their relatives the Levites made preparations for them.

16 The entire ministry to the Lord was prepared that day for observance of the
Passover and the sacrifice of burnt offerings on the altar of the Lord, as King Josiah

---

a   Literally, "Stand in the Holy Place by groupings of the father's households of your brothers the lay
people, according to the Levite divisions of father's households."

had ordered. [17] The Israelites who were present celebrated the Passover at that time and observed the Feast of Unleavened Bread for seven days. [18] The Passover had not been celebrated like that in Israel since the days of the prophet Samuel. None of the kings of Israel had celebrated the Passover like Josiah did—with the priests, the Levites, all Judah and *Northern* Israel who were present, and the inhabitants of Jerusalem. [19] This Passover was celebrated in the eighteenth year of Josiah's reign.

Josiah's Death at the Hand of Pharaoh Neco

[20] After all this, when Josiah had reestablished the temple, Neco king of Egypt went up to Carchemish on the Euphrates River for battle. Josiah went out to meet him *in battle.* [21] But Neco sent messengers saying, "What *fight* is there between you and me, O King of Judah? I am not going up *to fight* against you today but against the house *of the king of Assyria,* with which I am at war. And God has ordered me to hurry, so stop *opposing* God, who is with me—or he will destroy you!"

[22] But Josiah would not turn his face away from Neco, so he disguised himself and went into battle. He didn't listen to the words of Neco from the mouth of God, so he went to fight him at the Megiddo Valley. [23] When archers shot King Josiah, he ordered his servants, "Take me away! I am badly wounded." [24] His servants took him out of his chariot, put him in his second chariot, and brought him to Jerusalem, where he died. He was buried in the tombs of his ancestors, and all Judah and Jerusalem mourned for Josiah. [25] Jeremiah sang a lament over Josiah. All the male and female singers speak of Josiah in their laments to this day. These became a tradition in Israel—take a look, they're recorded in the *Book of* Lamentations.

[26] The rest of the acts of Josiah, all the faithful things he did according to the Law of the LORD, [27] and his acts from beginning to end—take a look, they're recorded in the book Kings of Israel and Judah.

36 *2 Chronicles*

Jehoahaz' Short Reign Ended by Pharaoh

[1] The people of the land took Jehoahaz son of Josiah and made him king in Jerusalem in his father's place. [2] Jehoahaz was twenty-three years old when he became king, and he reigned for three months in Jerusalem. [3] Then the king of Egypt deposed him from *reigning over* Jerusalem and imposed a levy on the land *of Judah* of seventy-five hundred pounds of silver and seventy-five pounds[a] of gold. [4] The king of Egypt made Eliakim, Jehoahaz' brother, king over Judah and Jerusalem and changed his name to Jehoiakim. Neco seized Eliakim's brother *Jehoahaz* and took him to Egypt.

Jehoiakim's Evil Reign over Judah

[5] Jehoiakim was twenty-five years old when he became king, and he reigned for eleven years in Jerusalem. He did evil in the eyes of the LORD his God. [6] Nebuchadnezzar king of Babylon came up against Jehoiakim, bound him with bronze shackles, and took him to Babylon. [7] Nebuchadnezzar took some of the utensils of the temple of the LORD to Babylon and put them in his temple in Babylon.

---

a   Literally, "100 talents" and "a talent," respectively.

[8] The rest of the acts of Jehoiakim, the abominations he did and what was found against him—take a look, they're recorded in the book Kings of Israel and Judah. His son Jehoiachin reigned in his place.

Jehoiachin's Short, Evil Reign over Judah

[9] Jehoiachin was eighteen[a] years old when he became king, and he reigned three months and ten days in Jerusalem. He did evil in the eyes of the Lord. [10] At the turn of the year,[b] King Nebuchadnezzar sent messengers and had him brought to Babylon, along with the precious articles from the temple of the Lord. He made Jehoiachin's uncle[c] Zedekiah king over Judah and Jerusalem.

Zedekiah's Evil Reign over Judah Under Nebuchadnezzar

[11] Zedekiah was twenty-one years old when he became king, and he reigned for eleven years in Jerusalem. [12] He did evil in the eyes of the Lord his God; he did not humble himself before Jeremiah the prophet who spoke from the mouth of the Lord. [13] He also rebelled against King Nebuchadnezzar, who had made him swear *allegiance* by God. But he stiffened his neck and hardened his heart against turning to the Lord God of Israel. [14] In addition, the leading priests and the people were very unfaithful, *performing* all the abominations of the *pagan* nations. They defiled the temple of the Lord that he had consecrated in Jerusalem. [15] The Lord, the God of their ancestors, sent *word* to them by his messengers again and again, for he had compassion on his people and on his dwelling place. [16] But they scorned the messengers of God, despised his words, and mocked his prophets, until the wrath of the Lord rose against his people, until *there was* no remedy.

Destruction of Jerusalem

[17] So he brought the king of the Babylonians against them, who killed their young men with the sword in the house of their sanctuary. He had no compassion on young men or women, the elderly, or the weak. He gave them all into his hand. [18] He took to Babylon all the articles of the temple of God, great and small, the treasures of the temple of the Lord, and the treasures of the king and his officials. [19] They burned the temple of God and tore down the wall of Jerusalem. They burned all the great houses in the fire and destroyed all its precious articles. [20] Those who escaped the sword he took into exile in Babylon. They became slaves to him and to his sons until the kingdom of Persia came to power. [21] This was to fulfill the word of the Lord *given* through the mouth of Jeremiah, until the land had enjoyed its Sabbaths. All the days it lay desolate it kept the Sabbath *rest*, until the seventy years *prophesied* were fulfilled.[d]

---

a From the Septuagint and 2 Kings 24:8; Masoretic text: "eight."
b The Jewish year begins in spring.
c From the Septuagint and 2 Kings 24:17; Masoretic text: "brother."
d See Jeremiah 25:11.

Cyrus Orders Restoration of the Temple

²² In the first year of Cyrus king of Persia,ᵃ to fulfill the word of the LORD throughᵇ Jeremiah, the LORD stirred up the spirit of Cyrus king of Persia to proclaim thisᶜ throughout all his kingdom (and *put it* in writing):

> ²³ **Cyrus King of Persia**
> **Proclamation**
>
> The LORD God of heaven has given me all the kingdoms of the earth. He has appointed me to build a temple for him in Jerusalem, which is in Judah. Whoever is among you of all his people, may the LORD your God be with you. Let that person go up *to Jerusalem.*

---

a   About 539 BC.
b   Literally, "by the mouth of."
c   Literally, "to make a voice pass."

Historical Books Glossary

Abomination	Something disgusting, horrible, shameful, and detestable.
Amen	A transliteration from the Hebrew *amen*, which means "so be it." It is an expression of affirmation, total agreement. In Greek it may also carry the meaning of "truly," "indeed," or "may it be fulfilled."
Anakites a.k.a. Sons of Anak	Descendants of Anak, related to the Rephaites, who inhabited parts of Canaan when the Israelites arrived. Israel defeated them except for those in Gaza, Gad, and Ashdod.
Anoint	To pour or smear oil (commonly olive oil) upon someone. In religious life this is done as part of a religious ceremony upon a person's appointment to a ministry (e.g., priesthood) as a symbol of the divine transfer of powers and/or authority and/or responsibility. In ancient secular life, anointing was done for many reasons: to get relief from the sun, to promote healing, as part of infant care, to attend to one's appearance, or to honor a guest upon entering the house. The dead were anointed with perfume to help ameliorate the odor of decay.
Apostasy	To turn away from the Lord.
Arabah	Hebrew for "a desert, dry place." In Scripture the term refers to the depression that runs from the Sea of Galilee south to the Gulf of Aqaba. The Northern Arabah runs from the Sea of Galilee to the Dead Sea. The Southern Arabah runs from the Dead Sea to the Gulf of Aqaba. Since the formation of today's nation of Israel, the term refers to the area south of the Dead Sea at the Israel/Jordan border.
Aram	An area encompassing northern Canaan and today's Syria. Several independent city-states rose up within it. Because Damascus was the best known and most successful of these, it is sometimes referred to as Aram.
Aramaic	A Semitic language closely related to Hebrew. It became the language of region-wide communication by the eighth century BC, the time of King Hezekiah and the prophet Isaiah.
Are/is to	See "Shall."
Ascribe	Credit a person with having.
Asherah	A Canaanite goddess, the mother of Baal. The Hebrew term is also used for the cult objects that were used in her worship: poles (similar to totem poles) and/or trees that were set up near altars.
Atonement	At-one-ment. When two persons, usually God and a human, come back into harmonious relationship because the person who offended has paid for their offense(s). Regarding sin against God, in the Old Testament, the payment was made through the sacrificial system. The priests "made atonement" by offering to God the sacrifices the Israelites brought.
Baal	The Canaanite storm god and the male god of fertility. In Canaanite mythology, Baal had intercourse every year with Ashtaroth, the goddess of fertility, which made the crops grow. Each region had its own god (e.g., Baal of Peor, meaning the one worshiped on Mount Peor).

Blaspheme	To slander or defame a person by falsehood. To blaspheme God is similar, although the consequences are infinitely more serious. It includes many kinds of acts, from cursing God to slighting God (i.e., taking him lightly, as of little account).
Bless, blessed	God toward people: to watch over, protect, bestow spiritual prosperity (holiness) or material prosperity (e.g., "God will bless us.").
	People toward God: to declare approval and support. To praise and/or honor and worship as good (e.g., "I will bless the Lord.").
	People toward people: to provide a benefit or meet a person's need or to call upon God for his care of someone (e.g., "May God bless you.").
Blessing	Verb: the act of asking God to bless.
	Noun: the spiritual or material prosperity or happiness resulting from being blessed.
Bowed down	A range of actions that all include bending the knee(s) and bowing the head by an inferior person toward their superior. It was the normal gesture by which one acknowledged the lordship of the person before them.
Bread	The Hebrew word for "bread," *lechem*, may also mean "food."
Burn, burn up	In the context of a sacrifice, "burn" has the meaning of offering something up to God. The verb could be rendered "offer up," "offer up in smoke," or "offer by fire."
Burnt offering	An offering to God, part of which was burned up. See "Sacrifice."
Call upon the name of the Lord	To invoke the name of the Lord in worship and/or prayer.
Canaan	Roughly, today's Lebanon, Israel, Palestinian territories, the western part of Jordan, and southwestern Syria. The exact borders are given in Numbers 34:3–12; however, some of the locations cited are uncertain.
Canaanite	"Canaanite" was used in a broad sense to include all the tribes living in the land west of the Jordan River that were occupied by Israel after their conquest. It was used in a narrower sense to refer to a specific tribe.
Circumcision	The cutting off of a male's foreskin. It is a sign of the Israelite's purification and commitment to a covenantal relationship with God. Under the Mosaic law, all male children were to be circumcised on the eighth day of their life. See Genesis 17:10–14 and Leviticus 12:3. It also means "circumcision of the heart" (removing the foreskin of the heart).
City	In the first two millennia BC, cities in Israel were seldom larger than five thousand people and typically much smaller. In *The Readable Bible*, "town" refers to communities of a hundred to a thousand families. "Village" refers to smaller communities; however, the population information is uncertain.
City gate	Where community leaders (elders, judges, etc.) sat in judgment and citizens gathered for public business, conversation, and fellowship. Because the city gate controlled who could enter or leave, and since it was where residents gathered and officials met the people, the term became a symbol for control of the city.

Clan	A number of families under a common leader and with a common ancestor. Several clans may be in a tribe.
Clean, unclean	These terms refer to whether a person, animal, or inanimate object fits God's conditions for use by his people in their daily lives or in his prescribed ceremonies. The terms do not necessarily refer to sinfulness or hygiene, although they sometimes do. Persons and objects became unclean primarily through contact with unclean persons or things. Animals were categorized as clean or unclean in the first five books of the Bible.
Concubine	A female sexual partner who lives under a man's care but is not his wife.
Consecrate	To set something apart for God or his service.
Covenant	A solemn agreement that binds the parties to one another in a permanent, defined relationship. It may define the obligations of a superior to an inferior and the reverse, or it may define the mutual obligations of equals. The term sometimes refers to the stone tablets with the Ten Commandments inscribed on them, and sometimes to the covenant relationship of God with Israel, under which they were to obey his laws and he was to be their provider and protector.
Cush	The region south of Egypt; today's Eritrea, Sudan, and Ethiopia.
Defile	To make dirty, corrupt, and/or ceremonially unclean (and therefore unfit for God's people or for use in God's work).
Daughter of [location]	An expression meant to evoke a sense of pride and affection in the natives of that place, just as one should have toward their own daughter.
Desert	A dry, sandy region. See "Wilderness." Deserts may have wilderness areas.
Despise	Regard with contempt, loathe.
Detestable	See "Abomination."
Divination	Getting information by occult ritual (e.g., contact with supernatural spirits, reading so-called signs that indicate future events).
Drink offering	An offering made by pouring wine on the sanctuary floor.
Ephod	A closely fitted embroidered outer vest.
Ephraim	A tribe of Israel named after the younger son of Joseph, adopted by Jacob. It became one of the largest tribes in Israel. Sometimes "Ephraim" is used as a metaphor for Northern Israel and sometimes for the whole nation.
Eunuch	A castrated person, usually an official of the royal court.
Fear	With reference to God, regard with deep reverence, respect, and awe.
Fell on his face/ before him/ to the ground	All three terms refer to lying facedown or kneeling before someone with one's hands on the ground, putting one's body in a reverential/yielded position as a gesture of submission and worship.
Fellowship offering	A.k.a. "peace offering" and "wave offering." A sacrificial offering that was lifted and swung back and forth before the Lord. Then it became the property of the priests.

Festival	A period of "sacred assembly" for commemoration and/or celebration. Traditionally, festivals have been referred to as "feasts." Today "feast" is used primarily to refer to a large, elaborate meal, whereas "festival" includes much more than that, and may not include a meal at all. Thus, "festival" communicates the biblical concept more accurately. See "The Festivals of the Lord" table in the back of the book.
Firstfruits	The first and most highly valued part of the harvest. Metaphorically, it is the first of something which represents that there is more to come (e.g., Christ was the firstfruit of all believers—those who will be raised from the dead).
Flock	A group of goats or sheep.
Follow	In the context of rules and regulations, "follow," "keep," "observe," and "obey" all mean to adhere to, to abide by, or to act in accordance with.
Food	See "Bread."
Foreigner	Permanent non-Israelite residents among the Israelites, or travelers, or nomads who would appear periodically among the Israelites.
Freewill offering	A spontaneous offering of praise to the Lord—one not made for atonement or to fulfill a vow.
Glean	To gather the crop, usually grain, the harvesters left behind.
Glory of God/of the Lord	The all-encompassing majesty of God that cannot be fully comprehended by humans (e.g., his lovingkindness, power, all-knowing presence, creativity, etc.). The display of God's presence and character that can be seen in his creation, his acts, and in his presence when he shows himself visibly (as light, fire, or in some other form).
Grain offering	An offering of flour mixed with olive oil and frankincense. See Leviticus 2.
Hebrew	The term's origin is uncertain. Abraham and his descendants through Jacob are known as Hebrews.
Herd	A group of cattle or other large animals.
High place	A site of pagan worship, usually an elevated location.
High priest	See "Priest."
Holy, become/ keep	Set apart for the purpose(s) or service of God. An object that is holy can be used only for God's purposes, usually in a ritual or sacrifice, or for consumption by the priests. Like a day that is holy, a person who is holy is one who has been set apart for God's purposes.
Holy Place	The area inside the tabernacle in front of the Most Holy Place. Lowercase, "a holy place" refers to the area inside the tabernacle curtains. God also occasionally designated other places as holy, such as the area around the burning bush in Exodus 3:5.
Horn	Metaphorically, a symbol of strength, power.
Horsemen	Cavalrymen and/or charioteers and/or those who took care of their horses.
House of	The term may refer to a person's immediate family, his immediate and extended family, or to all of them and their servants or household staff.
Idol	A carved, cast metal, or pottery image believed to be a deity, or a cult object related to the worship of a God.

Impale	Execute a person by placing them upon a stake that pierces their body. It is unclear whether the Hebrew verb *talah* refers to hanging or impaling.
Inheritance	The land of Israel given to Abraham and his seed as their inheritance (i.e., to be passed down). And God chose the Israelites as his inheritance (Psalms 28:9; 33:12).
Isaac	Abraham's second son; his only son by his wife Sarah.
Jacob	The original name for Isaac's second son (see Genesis 25:26). A metaphor for the Israelites (who are all descendants of Jacob, who was renamed "Israel" later in life).
Judah	The foremost tribe of Israel; the tribe of David, Solomon, and Jesus. It was named after its patriarch, the fourth son of Jacob. The name is often used as a metaphor for Israel.
	Upon the split of Israel into two kingdoms, its territory formed the bulk of the southern Kingdom of Judah.
Judge, to	In the historical books, to lead Israel and to decide upon matters for it.
Keep	See "Follow."
Kenite	A semi-nomadic tribe. Some of its clans allied with Israel.
Kerethites a.k.a. Carites	The Kerethites and Pelethites were members of David's army who remained loyal to him in times of crisis, and may have formed his bodyguard. "While speculations about the two groups abound, the origin of them is unknown.
King	A king was the ruler over a city and its surrounding territory, which sometimes would have been a relatively small area. See "City."
Law/law	"Law" may refer to any of these four things, depending upon context: – the Ten Commandments, – the entire first five books of the Bible (a.k.a. Pentateuch, Torah), – the first five books plus the oral tradition of unwritten laws that some Jews considered authoritative, or – a reference to all the Jewish Scriptures.
Lay down with ancestors	To die.
Leaven	Any substance (usually yeast) added to dough to make it rise by releasing gas into it, thereby lightening and softening the dough. Since a very small amount affects a large amount of dough, the word is sometimes used as a metaphor for a small thing that has a large effect (such as sin). See Galatians 5:9. Under the Old Testament law, Jews were forbidden to eat or have leaven or leavened bread in the home on certain holy days. See "Unleavened."
Levites	The descendants of Levi (Jacob's third son). They served at the tabernacle. Aaron (Moses' brother) and his descendants were Levites; as priests they were a subset of the Levites. Only they could offer sacrifices. The Levites who were not descendants of Aaron helped the priests and took care of the tabernacle.
Locust	Grasshopper in its swarming phase.

LORD	The name of God is four Hebrew letters represented in English by *YHWH*. Out of reverence for God's name, we render the word as "LORD." The Hebrew, *YHWH*, cannot be translated exactly, but it is probably derived from the word "to be."
Lord GOD/ Lord my GOD/ Sovereign LORD	When "Yahweh" appears after *Adonai* (a Hebrew term of reverence for God), we usually render the two words as "Lord GOD." However, because these are synonymous terms next to each other, one reinforcing the other, they can equally well be rendered "Sovereign LORD." The Readable Bible rendering depends on the context.
of Armies	Traditionally, "LORD of Hosts." While "hosts" refers to heavenly bodies, the term rendered "hosts" literally is "armies." However, there is some debate as to whether "armies" should sometimes be taken in a general sense (e.g., "What an army of people") rather than in a military sense. Metaphorically, the term "hosts/armies" can be reflected back upon God, resulting in the term rendered "Sovereign LORD" in some Bibles.
Lord, my lord	Terms of respect used by a person of lower rank when addressing a person of higher rank.
Lovingkindness	Steadfast, faithful, loyal love; full of kindness and mercy. Hebrew: *chesed*.
Meeting tent	The portable dwelling place for God's presence within the Israelite camp (also called the tabernacle of the covenant or simply, the tabernacle). Before the tabernacle was constructed, Moses met with God in a meeting tent outside the camp. It was replaced by permanent structures (sequentially).
Midianites	A nomadic people from east of the Gulf of Aqaba. Those referenced in the book of Numbers lived somewhere east of the Jordan River and had allied themselves with the Moabites.
Molech	A god worshiped in Canaan, sometimes by the sacrifice of children.
Most Holy Place	The area behind the veil inside the tabernacle, where God's presence dwelled over the ark of the covenant. Also known as the "Holy of Holies."
Mount Horeb	Another name for Mount Sinai.
Mount Sinai	The mountain where Moses received the Ten Commandments and other laws from God. It may or may not be where today's Mount Sinai is located, in Egypt at the southern end of the Sinai Peninsula.
Mount Zion	In the historical books, the term refers to the City of David, the southernmost part of Jerusalem. In the prophetic books, the term refers to the mount upon which the temple stood.
Must	See "Shall."
Negev	A dry, mostly mountainous region from the dunes of the Mediterranean to the Dead Sea valley, from between Hebron and Beersheba south to its apex at modern-day Eilat on the Gulf of Aqaba. Though called a desert, it has areas of fertile soil with a foot of yearly rainfall (barely enough to grow a crop in a favorable year). The term can also denote "south."
New wine	Freshly pressed grape juice, unfermented.
Northern Israel	The Readable Bible text inserts "*Northern*" before "Israel" when the reference is clearly to the northern kingdom, that of the tribes north of the land of the tribe of Judah.

Obey	See "Follow."
Observe	See "Follow."
Offering	See "Sacrifice."
Oil	Usually from olives. Used as a healing, soothing substance and for cooking and anointing. See "Anoint."
Oracle	A message from a supernatural power given through another person.
Ordinances	See "Regulations."
Ox	A castrated bull. Castration makes bulls easier to control and, therefore, to use for labor such as pulling plows and carts.
Pagan	Follower of a polytheistic religion (i.e., one who believes in many gods).
Passover	The annual celebration of Israel's departure from bondage in Egypt brought about by God killing all the firstborn of Egypt and passing over the firstborn of Israel. See Exodus 12 and Numbers 9.
Pass [person] through the fire	It is unknown whether this expression refers to a symbolic act or is a euphemism for making a human sacrifice."
Peace	Hebrew: *shalom*. A sense of wholeness, well-being free from disturbance.
Peace offering	See "Fellowship Offering."
Pelethites	See "Kerethites."
Pharaoh	A title of the king of Egypt.
Priest	A mediator between God and his people, a spokesman for God. Jewish priests, descendants of Moses' brother Aaron, (a) taught the law, (b) handled the temple administration, and (c) received on behalf of God the sacrifices brought to the temple. See "Levites."
High priest a.k.a. chief priest	Literally, "the anointed priest." As the highest-ranking priest, he had special garments (see Exodus 28:1–43; 39:2–31) and, among other special duties, on the annual Day of Atonement he was the only priest allowed to enter the Most Holy Place to atone for the guilt of the sins of Israel. Sometimes the office was shared. A retired chief priest was also addressed as and referred to as a chief priest.
Prince	A tribal ruler or leader; not necessarily the son of a king.
Prophecy	That which has been spoken on God's behalf. Sometimes an act of prophecy involves the foretelling of something that will occur in the future.
Redeem	To pay a specified amount to be released from an obligation, to be delivered from a controlling power, or to recover ownership of something that was given to, claimed by, or dedicated to God.
Regulations	Regulations, rules, and stipulations are terms for actions that are either required or forbidden by God. Common terms in English translations include decrees, judgments, laws, ordinances, rules, regulations, stipulations, and statutes. The terms are basically synonymous.
Reproach	Noun: a cause of disgrace or shame. Verb: to bring into discredit or to point out someone as a cause of disgrace or shame.

Righteous/ righteousness	In secular life, to be righteous is to act with integrity with regard to what is right, to have high moral and ethical standards. In the Bible, righteousness is the state of being that God intends for people. A righteous person is one whose life is in conformity with the inner character and standards of God. One who is righteous acts in accordance with God's law as written in the Bible and written upon the heart of the believer. The Bible teaches that God makes righteous those who follow him (i.e., who put their faith in Jesus Christ as their Lord and Savior).
Rules	See "Regulations."
Sackcloth	Very rough cloth used primarily for grain sacks. It was also made into crude, coarse clothing that was worn to afflict the wearer and show others they were mourning on account of the loss of a loved one or other tragedy, or to show they were in a state of repentance on account of sin. Oftentimes mourners also threw ashes upon themselves (hence the familiar phrase "sackcloth and ashes").
Sacred	Set apart for the purpose(s) and/or service of God. See "Holy."
Sacrifice	Jerusalem in AD 70, a gift/offering to God, often presented to him by burning it. It was offered to express appreciation for what God had done for the offerer or to appease God for the offerer's sin (see Leviticus 1–7).

The owner made the offering as an act of faith, believing that the Lord will accept it as an outward sign of their inward belief in him, their acceptance of his lordship, and their desire to be in a harmonious relationship with him. |
Salvation	In the Old Testament, deliverance in battle or from evil people. Or, peace with God realized through a right relationship with him, a relationship entered into through faith in God that results in (1) the forgiveness of a person's sins and (2) the heartfelt desire and capability to serve him.
Sanctify	To make holy, morally pure. See "Holy" and "Consecrate."
Sanctuary	The place set aside for God's service. Sometimes it refers to the Most Holy Place and sometimes to the whole area within the courtyard border.
Seir	The country around the Seir Highlands, southeast of the Dead Sea.
Selah	The meaning of this Hebrew term is uncertain. It is generally believed to be a musical notation (e.g., interlude, repeat). Since its meaning is uncertain and it adds nothing meaningful to Scripture, we present it in light text at the right-hand margin.
Septuagint	A Greek translation of the Old Testament written in the third and second centuries BC. The translation philosophy and quality varies by section. Its Pentateuch is quite literal and accurate. The Historical Books and Prophets are a more relaxed translation, and the Wisdom Literature and Poetical Books have some very loosely translated parts. Nevertheless, it was the Bible used in New Testament times. Almost every New Testament quotation of the Old Testament is from it.
Shall	"Shall," "is/are to," and "must" are used to indicate a command or to emphatically state a fact (e.g., "The Lord shall reign forever"). "Will" is used to point to a future event or condition.

Shekel	A measure of weight and value. About 0.37 troy ounces (11.5 grams), about the weight of two American nickels or two twenty-cent euro coins.
Sheol	The place of the dead. Sometimes the term refers to a person's grave or to death in general.
Shiloh	An important city about twenty miles north-northeast of Jerusalem that was a prominent center of worship in the time of the judges. It lost its significance soon afterward. The ark of the covenant resided there during the time of the judges and throughout Samuel's lifetime.
Sons of men	A metaphor for mankind.
Soul	The Hebrew term translated as "soul," *nephesh*, may also be rendered as a personal pronoun. For example, "*nephesh* sings" can be rendered "my soul sings" or "I sing."
Statutes	See "Regulations."
Stiff-necked	Stubborn, haughty in one's obstinacy. Derived from the picture of a beast of burden refusing to be directed by its master.
Swear	Solemnly promise; promise with an oath.
Tarshish	Mentioned in Scripture as a major trading place with a fleet of ships and as a source of minerals. Whether Tarshish is a trading destination and/or a city or place is unknown. Probably it is in modern-day Spain or perhaps Tunisia. The designation "ships of Tarshish" meant well-built vessels that could be sailed over journeys of hundreds of miles in open water, rather than smaller, commuter vessels that stayed within sight of land.
Thummim	See "Urim and Thummim."
Tithe	One-tenth of what is produced or earned. Given by the Israelites as an offering to God.
Town	See "City."
Trans-Euphrates	The provinces west of the Euphrates River. The boundaries varied over time. The term, at that time, referred to the land ruled by Assyria, Babylon, or Persia.
Transgression	Failure to fulfill a command, law, or duty.
Tribe	One of the twelve tribes of Israel (Reuben, Simeon, Judah, Dan, Naphtali, Gad, Asher, Issachar, Zebulun, Benjamin, Ephraim, and Manasseh), descendants of eleven of Jacob's twelve sons. Rather than possess land and farm, Levi's sons served as priests, tabernacle attendants, and teachers. Joseph's sons Ephraim and Manasseh were each established as a full tribe to complete the number twelve (see Genesis 48:5).
Unclean	See "Clean, unclean."
Unleavened	Made without yeast or any other leavening agent. Unleavened bread is flat, tough, and chewy or crisp. It was a sign of poverty and/or temporariness. See "Leaven."
Wadi	A water-worn ravine or other depression that is usually dry.
Wave offering	See "Fellowship Offering."

Wilderness	An uninhabited area with desertlike characteristics, though not necessarily sandy. It is sometimes mountainous, often with terraces and steep cliffs from highlands to ravines more than a thousand feet below.
Winnow	To toss crushed grain kernels in the air, so the bits of dirt and husk will be separated from the heavier, edible parts.
Yahweh	See "Lord."
Zion	At first, a Jebusite city on a high point, Mount Zion. After David captured the city, Jerusalem was built upon it. Zion is sometimes a metaphor for Jerusalem and sometimes a metaphor for Israel.

Weights and Measures in Chronicles

Read about biblical weights and measures in "Translation Notes."

Length	
Cubit	From the elbow to the end of the fingers, about eighteen inches.
Handbreadth	Three inches.
Weight	
Shekel	About 0.4 avoirdupois ounce, about the weight of two American nickels or two twenty-cent euro coins. A shekel may also refer to a silver coin of the same weight.
Talent	About seventy-five pounds.
Capacity – Dry	
Cor	6½ bushels.
Capacity – Liquid	
Bath	Six gallons.

Map Notes

The exact routes the fighting forces took are unknown. Readable Bible battle maps assume the forces took the easiest and most direct routes, through lowlands and passes whenever possible, using high points to hide forces. The maps provide a feel for the battle movements, not the exact movements.

When maps show the location of people groups (e.g., Amorites, Ammonites), the location(s) shown are in the context of the year and place of the events. Some people groups had more than one location, and some moved. Thus, a group may appear in different locations on different maps.

Likewise, there are many cases of two or more cities having the same name. Maps show the city location related to the referenced text. When city locations are in doubt, two locations with the same name may appear on a map.

The exact routes the fighting forces took are unknown. Readable Bible battle maps assume the forces took the easiest and most direct routes, through lowlands and passes whenever possible, using high points to hide forces. The maps provide a feel for the battle movements, not the exact movements.

FAMILIAR VERSES

Familiar Verses in 1 Chronicles

16:25–26	[25] The LORD is great and greatly to be praised; he is to be feared above all gods. [26] For all the gods of other people are only idols, but the LORD made the heavens.
28:9b	The LORD searches all hearts and understands every purpose and thought.
29:14	Who am I, and who are my people that we should be able to give willingly like this? For everything is from you, and we have given you only what comes from your hand.

Familiar Verses in 2 Chronicles

1:7	That night God appeared to Solomon in a dream and said, "Ask me—what shall I give you?"
1:11–12	[11] God answered Solomon, "Because this is in your heart, and because you did not ask for riches, wealth, honor, or the death of your enemies, or even long life, but you have asked for wisdom and understanding that you may govern my people over whom I have made you king, [12] wisdom and understanding are given to you. I am also giving you wealth, riches, and honor such as no king before you has had and above any king after you shall have."
6:18	But will God really dwell on earth with humans? Look, the heavens, even the highest heavens cannot contain you! How much less can this temple I have built!
7:14	If my people, who are called by my name, will humble themselves, pray, seek my face, and turn from their wicked ways, then I will hear from heaven, forgive their sins, and heal their land.
15:2b	If you seek him, he will be found by you. But if you abandon him, he will abandon you.
16:9a	The eyes of the LORD range about throughout the whole earth, that he may strongly support those who are wholeheartedly devoted to him.
32:7b–8a	[7b] He who is with you is greater than those who are with him. [8a] With him is only the arm of flesh, but the LORD our God is with us to help us and fight our battles.

PEOPLE LIST

People in 1 Chronicles

Name	Key Facts	Events	Chapter
Aaron	First high priest	His descendants transported the ark and served in the temple.	6, 15, 23–24, 27
Abiathar	Priest	Carried the ark to Jerusalem	15
Abihu	Second son of Aaron the priest	Died before his father and had no sons	24
Abinadab	From Kiriath Jearim	Kept the ark at his house	13
Abishai	Joab's brother, chief of David's mighty men	Killed three hundred; honored doubly Struck down 18,000 Edomites Defeated the Ammonites	11 18 19
Abraham	First patriarch of Israel	Descendants listed Mentioned	1 16, 29
Adam	First man	Descendants listed	1
Aharhel		Clans listed	1
Ahimelech	Priest who assisted David in organizing the divisions	Mentioned	24
Ahio	Abinadab's son	Led the cart with the ark of God	13
Amasai	A leader of David's fighting men	Prophesied peace to David	12
Araunah a.k.a. Ornan	A Jebusite	Owned threshing floor David bought to stop the plague	21
Asaph	Head of the musicians, prophet under David	Assigned to give thanks to the Lord Mentioned	15–16 25–26
Asher	Jacob's eighth son	Descendants listed	7
Beerah	Reubenite leader	Exiled to Assyria	5
Benaiah	Son of Jehoiada, a leader of David's fighting men and head of his bodyguard	Struck down two champions of Moab, a lion and a seven-foot soldier Mentioned	11 18
Benjamin	Jacob's twelfth son	Descendants listed	7–8
Caleb	Brought back a good report when sent to explore the promised land	Descendants listed	2

David	Israel's greatest king	Descendants listed	3
		Anointed king after Saul's death; captured Jerusalem	11
		Feared God when Uzzah was killed; sent ark to Obed-Edom's house	13
		Defeated the Philistines	14
		Danced as ark brought back to Jerusalem	15
		Victorious against several cities; dedicated precious metals to the Lord	18
		Defeated Ammon and Gath	20
		Incited by Satan to take a census; after God struck Israel with a plague, built an altar and made sacrifices to stop it	21
		Commanded Solomon to build a temple for the Lord; provided plans and materials	22, 28–29
		Made Solomon king	23
		Mentioned	26
Eleazar	Son of Dodai, one of the three mighty men of David	Struck down Philistines with David at Pas Dammim	11
Eleazar	Third son of Aaron the priest	Served as priest; sixteen leaders were among his descendants	24
Elhanan	Son of Jair	Stuck down Lahmi, brother of Goliath	20
Gad	Prophet, David's seer	Sent to David with three choices of how to appease God's wrath after the census	21
		Mentioned	29
Hadadezer	King of Zobah	David defeated him and seized his gold weapons and bronze to make temple articles.	18
Hadoram*a*	Son of King Tou of Hamath	Sent to David to bless him with gold, silver, and bronze	18
Hanun	Son of King Nahash	David showed him kindness when his father died, but he humiliated David's servants.	19
Heman	King David's seer, songleader	Mentioned	6
		Along with his children, sang and played instruments in the temple	15–16, 25
Hiram	King of Tyre	Sent David building materials for his palace	14
Isaac	Patriarch of Israel	Mentioned	16, 29
Issachar	Jacob's ninth son	Descendants listed	7
Ithamar	Fourth son of Aaron the priest	Served as priest; eight leaders were among his descendants	24
Jabez	More honorable than his brothers	God answered his request to bless him and enlarge his territory.	4

a   A.k.a. Joram (2 Samuel 8:10).

Jacob	Third patriarch of Israel, ancestor of the twelve tribes	Descendants listed Mentioned	2 16
Jashobeam	A Hacmonite, head over David's fighting men	Killed three hundred at one time	11
Jeduthun	Prophesied with musical instruments	Along with his children, sang and played instruments in the temple	16, 25
Joab	David's army commander	Mentioned Defeated the Arameans Destroyed Ammon	18 19 20
Jonathan	Son of Shimea, brother of David	Struck down a huge man with twenty-four fingers and toes	20
Judah	Jacob's fourth son, ancestor of Jesus Christ	Descendants listed	2, 4
Lahmi	Brother of Goliath	Struck down by Elhanan	20
Levi	Jacob's third son from whom the Levites descended	Descendants listed	6, 23
Manasseh	Joseph's first son, adopted by Jacob and made a half-tribe	Descendants listed	7
Michal	David's wife and Saul's daughter	Despised David when he danced as the ark was brought to Jerusalem	15
Moses	Led Israel out of Egypt and received the law from God	Mentioned	6, 15, 21–23, 26
Nadab	First son of Aaron the priest	Died before his father and had no sons	24
Nahash	King of Ammon	Kind to David	19
Naphtali	Jacob's sixth son	Descendants listed	7
Nathan	Prophet of the Lord	Told David he would not build God's house but his son would Mentioned	17 29
Obed-Edom	A Gittite	Blessed when he kept the ark of God at his house for three months Ark picked up from his house	13 15
Reuben	Jacob's first son	Descendants listed	5
Samuel	Prophet of Israel	Anointed David king Mentioned	11 29

Saul	First king of Israel	Mentioned	5
		Descendants listed	9
		Died on the battlefield and Philistines hung his skull in idol temple.	10
		Mentioned	10–12, 17, 26
Shemaiah	Son of Nethanel the scribe	Recorded names and duty assignments for Levites	24
Shophach	Commander of King Hadadezer's army	Killed in battle against David and his army	19
Sibbecai	A Hushathite	Struck down Sippai, subduing the Philistines	20
		Mentioned	27
Simeon	Jacob's second son	Descendants listed	4
Sippai	A descendant of the Rephaim	Struck down by Sibbecai	20
Solomon	King of Israel, David's son	Mentioned	18
		Commanded by David to build God's temple	22, 28
		Became king over Israel	23
		Chosen as next king	28
Tiglath-Pileser a.k.a. Pul	King of Assyria	Took the Reubenites, Gadites, and half-tribe of Manasseh into exile	5
Tou	King of Hamath	Sent his son to David with gold, silver, and bronze articles	18
Uzzah	Abinadab's son	Died when he touched the ark	13
Zadok	Priest who assisted David in organizing the divisions	Carried the ark to Jerusalem	15
		Mentioned	24

People in 2 Chronicles

Name	Key Facts	Events	Chapter
Aaron	First high priest of Israel	Mentioned	13, 26, 29, 31, 35
Abdon	Son of Micah	Josiah sent him to inquire of the Lord.	34
Abijah	King of Judah, son of Rehoboam and Maacah	Rehoboam made him head over his brothers, intending to make him king.	11
		Reigned as king after Rehoboam's death	12
		Victorious against Israel	13
Abijah	Mother of King Hezekiah	Mentioned	29
Abraham	Patriarch of Israel	Mentioned	20, 30

Adonijah	Levite under King Jehoshaphat	Taught God's law to Judah	17
Ahab	King of Israel	Made alliance with Jehoshaphat	18
		Counseled by four hundred lying prophets; killed in battle	
		Mentioned	21–22
Ahaz	King of Judah, son of Jotham	Became king after Jotham's death	27
		Rebelled against God, worshiped idols and sacrificed his children	28
		The Lord gave him over to Aram and Israel.	28
		He asked Assyria for help and gave them treasure from the temple.	28
Ahaziah	King of Israel	Made alliance with Jehoshaphat	20
Ahaziah a.k.a. Jehoahaz	King of Judah, youngest son of Jehoram	Only son not killed by raiders	21
		Did evil in the Lord's eyes; allied with Israel to fight Aram; executed by Jehu	22
Ahijah	A Shilonite and prophet	Mentioned	9–10
Ahikam	Son of Shaphan	Josiah sent him to inquire of the Lord.	34
Amariah	Chief priest	Appointed over Jehoshaphat for matters concerning the Lord	19
Amasa	Son of Hadlai, Ephraim leader	Urged troops to return Judah's captives	28
Amaziah	King of Judah, son of Joash	Reigned over Judah righteously at first	24–25
		Turned to idols; defeated by Israel; killed by assassins	25
		Mentioned	26
Amon	King of Judah, son of Manasseh	Did evil, sacrificing to idols; murdered by his servants	33
Asa	King of Judah, son of Rehoboam	Became king after Rehoboam's death; followed God, smashed idols, and built fortified cities; won all battles and seized plunder	13–15
		Covenanted with Aram to fight Israel but the Lord brought war; enraged, he died without seeking God again, even when ill.	16
		Mentioned	20–21
Asahel	Levite under Jehoshaphat	Taught God's law to Judah	17
Asaph	Head of the musicians	Led the musicians in praising the Lord	5
		Mentioned	29, 35
Asiah	King Josiah's servant	Josiah sent him to inquire of the Lord.	34

Athaliah	Mother of Ahaziah, king of Judah	Encouraged Ahaziah to act wickedly; tried to murder every royal child after the death of her son Ahaziah	22
		Killed by Jehoiada and supporters	23
Azariah	Brother of King Jehoram	Murdered by Jehoram	21
Azariah (#2)	Brother of King Jehoram	Murdered by Jehoram	21
Azariah	High priest during King Hezekiah's reign	Explained how the Lord had blessed them with tithes and offerings	31
Azariah	Priest during King Uzziah's reign	Warned Uzziah not to burn incense	26
Azariah	Son of Jehohanan, Ephraim leader	Urged troops to return Judah's captives	28
Azariah	Son of Jeroham	Made covenant with Jehoiada	23
Azariah	Son of Obed	Made covenant with Jehoiada	23
Azariah	Son of Oded, a prophet	Told Asa the Lord was with Judah	15
Azrikam	Leader of King Ahaz' palace guard	Killed by Zicri	28
Azubah	King Jehoshaphat's mother	Mentioned	20
Baasha	King of Israel	Built fortress of Ramah against Judah	16
Ben-Hadad	King of Aram	Made covenant with Asa to attack Israel	16
Ben-Hail	Official of King Jehoshaphat	Taught God's law to Judah	17
Berekiah	Son of Meshillemoth, Ephraim leader	Urged troops to return Judah's captives	28
Bezalel	Craftsman for the tabernacle	Mentioned	1
Cyrus	King of Persia	God appointed him to rebuild the temple in Jerusalem.	36
David	Israel's greatest king	Mentioned	1–13, 16–17, 21, 23–24, 27–30, 32–35
Eliezer	Son of Dodavahu	Prophesied that the Lord would come out against Jehoshaphat's works due to alliance with King Ahaziah	20

Elijah	Prophet of the Lord	Told Jehoram the Lord was striking him with an illness and taking away his wives, sons, and possessions	21
Elishama	Priest under Jehoshaphat	Taught God's law to Judah	17
Elishaphat	Son of Zicri	Made covenant with Jehoiada	23
Elkanah	Second to King Ahaz	Killed by Zicri	28
Hadoram[a]	In charge of Judah's forced labor	Stoned to death by Israel	10
Hanani	Prophet of the Lord	Prophesied war for King Asa because he relied on Aram for help; thrown in prison	16
Hananiah	Royal official under Uzziah	Mustered the troops	26
Heman	Musician leader	Led the musicians in praising the Lord Mentioned	5 35
Hezekiah	King of Judah, son of Ahaz	Became king Did right; restored the temple Restored Passover celebration Restored tithes and offerings Prayed for victory over Assyria Became sick and prayed for healing	28 29 30 31 32 32
Hezekiah	Son of Shallum, Ephraim leader	Urged troops to return Judah's captives	28
Hilkiah	High priest during King Josiah's reign	Josiah gave him the money to restore the temple. Found the book of the law; sent to inquire of the Lord Mentioned	34 34 35
Hiram	King of Tyre	Solomon asked him for a skilled craftsman and timber for the temple. Sent ships to Ophir to bring gold, wood, and jewels to Solomon	2 8
Huldah	Wife of Shallum, a prophetess	King Josiah's servants came to inquire of the Lord. She prophesied disaster but not during Josiah's lifetime.	34
Huram-Abi	Skilled craftsman and engraver from Tyre	King Hiram sent him to Solomon to oversee temple construction.	2, 4
Iddo	A prophet	Mentioned	9, 12–13
Isaac	Patriarch of Israel	Mentioned	30
Isaiah	Prophet of God, son of Amoz	Mentioned Prayed with Hezekiah for victory over Assyria	26 32

---

a   A.k.a. Adoniram (1 Kings 4:6) and Adoram (1 Kings 12:18).

Ishmael	Son of Jehohanan	Made covenant with Jehoiada	23
Jacob a.k.a. Israel	Patriarch of Israel	Mentioned	30
Jahaziel	Son of Zechariah, a prophet	Prophesied that the Lord would defeat Judah's enemies	20
Jeduthun	Musician leader	Led the musicians in praising the Lord Mentioned	5 35
Jehiel	Brother of King Jehoram	Murdered by Jehoram	21
Jehoaddan	Mother of Amaziah	Mentioned	25
Jehoahaz	King of Judah, son of Josiah	Taken to Egypt after reigning three months	36
Jehoiachin	King of Judah, son of Jehoiakim	Taken to Babylon after reigning three months	36
Jehoiada	Chief priest under King Joash	Mentioned Gathered supporters to crown Joash king of Judah; had Athaliah killed Found wives for Joash; oversaw temple renewal	22 23 24
Jehoiakim a.k.a. Eliakim	King of Judah, brother of Jehoahaz	Made king by Pharaoh Neco when Jehoahaz was taken to Egypt Taken to Babylon in shackles	36 36
Jehoram	King of Israel, son of Ahab	Fought against Aram with Ahaziah of Judah; wounded	22
Jehoram	King of Judah, son of Jehoshaphat	Murdered his brothers Lost all he owned and died a painful death	21 22
Jehoram	Priest under King Jehoshaphat	Taught God's law to Judah	17
Jehoshaphat	King of Judah, son of Asa	Walked in God's ways; taught the law to Judah Allied himself with Ahab against Ramoth Gilead; the Lord protected him in battle Returned to following God His ships destroyed when he allied himself with King Ahaziah of Israel	17 18 19 20
Jehosheba	Daughter of King Jehoram, wife of Jehoiada the priest	Hid Joash from Athaliah so he would not be killed	22
Jehozabad	Moabite official of King Joash	Killed Joash after he turned from the Lord	24
Jehu	Son of Hanani, a prophet	Warned Jehoshaphat of the Lord's anger for helping Ahab Mentioned	19 20

Jehu	Son of Nimshi	Sent by the Lord to execute judgment on Ahab's family; hunted Ahaziah and killed him	22
Jeiel	Secretary under King Uzziah	Mustered the troops	26
Jekoliah	Mother of King Uzziah	Mentioned	26
Jeremiah	Prophet of the Lord	Sang funeral song over King Josiah	35
		Tried to warn King Zedekiah to return to God; prophesied destruction until the land was repaid its Sabbaths and the temple was rebuilt by Cyrus	36
Jeroboam	Son of Nebat	Mentioned	9
		Representing Israel, offered to serve Rehoboam if he lightened their labor	10
		Mentioned	11–12
		Defeated by Abijah; struck down by the Lord and died	13
Jerusha	Mother of Jotham, daughter of Zadok	Mentioned	27
Joah	Son of Joahaz, the recorder	King Josiah sent him to repair the temple.	34
Joash	King Ahab's son	King Ahab told him to put Micaiah in prison.	18
Joash a.k.a. Jehoahaz	King of Israel, son of Jehu	Defeated Amaziah and Judah in battle; plundered the temple and palace	25
Joash	King of Judah, son of Ahaziah	Saved from death when Athaliah killed the royal family	22
		Crowned king; renewed the temple	23–24
		Turned from the Lord after Jehoiada's death; killed by his servants	24
		Mentioned	25
Josiah	King of Judah, son of Amon	Became king	33
		Cleansed Judah of idols; repaired the temple; restored the law; renewed the covenant	34
		Celebrated Passover; died fighting Neco, though the Lord warned him to stay away	35
Jotham	King of Judah, son of Uzziah	Acted rightly; built cities	26–27
Maacah	Mother of King Abijah	Mentioned	13
Maacah	Wife of Rehoboam, daughter of Absalom	Rehoboam loved her more than all his other wives and concubines.	11
		Removed as queen mother by King Asa due to idol worship	15

Maaseiah	City official under Josiah	King Josiah sent him to repair the temple.	34
Maaseiah	Officer under King Uzziah	Mustered the troops	26
Maaseiah	Son of Adaiah	Made covenant with Jehoiada	23
Maaseiah	Son of King Ahaz	Killed by Zicri	28
Manasseh	King of Judah, son of Hezekiah	Became king Did evil, worshiped idols, sacrificed his children, and practiced sorcery; carried to Babylon in chains; repented later and served the Lord	32 33
Micaiah	Official of King Jehoshaphat, prophet of the Lord	Taught God's law to Judah Prophesied disaster in battle to Ahab; thrown in jail	17 18
Michael	Brother of King Jehoram	Murdered by Jehoram	21
Moses	Led Israel out of Egypt and received the law from God	Mentioned	1, 24–25, 30, 35
Naamah	Rehoboam's Ammonite mother	Mentioned	12
Nathan	Prophet during King David's reign	Mentioned	9
Nathaniah	Levite under King Jehoshaphat	Taught God's law to Judah	17
Nebuchadnezzar	King of Babylon	Took King Jehoiakim to Babylon along with some temple utensils	36
Neco	Pharaoh of Egypt	Warned King Josiah away from battle, but he was killed when he wouldn't turn back Seized King Jehoahaz and took him to Egypt; made Jehoiakim king	35 36
Nethanel	Official of King Jehoshaphat	Taught God's law to Judah	17
Obadiah	Official of King Jehoshaphat	Taught God's law to Judah	17
Obed-Edom	Levite who cared for temple treasures	Mentioned	25
Oded	Prophet of the Lord	Warned Israel to return the captives from Judah	28
Ornan a.k.a. Araunah	Jebusite who sold David his threshing floor	Mentioned	3
Pekah	King of Israel, son of Remaliah	Defeated Judah in battle	28

Rehoboam	King of Israel, son of Solomon	Reigned after Solomon died	9
		Rejected the elders' counsel and spoke harshly to Jeroboam, dividing Israel and Judah; fled before being stoned	10
		Heeded God's command not to attack Israel; built many fortified cities	11
		Abandoned God's law and was attacked by Egypt. When he repented, God decided not to completely destroy him (i.e., his reign).	12
Sennacherib	King of Assyria	Invaded Judah; taunted the Lord; defeated and killed after Hezekiah prayed	32
Shaphan	Son of Azaliah, scribe	King Josiah sent him to repair the temple; read book of the Law to Josiah	34
Sheba, queen of		Came to Jerusalem to test Solomon's wisdom; impressed, she gave him spices, gold, and jewels; he gave her more in return	9
Shemaiah	Prophet of God	Told King Rehoboam not to attack Israel	11
		Prophesied that the Lord had given them over to Egypt due to disobedience	12
		Taught God's law to Judah	17
Shemiramoth	Levite under King Jehoshaphat	Taught God's law to Judah	17
Shephatiah	Brother of King Jehoram	Murdered by Jehoram	21
Shishak	King of Egypt	Attacked Judah	12
Solomon	King of Israel, David's son	God appeared to him and asked what he wanted. He asked for wisdom and also received wealth, riches, and honor.	1
		Built the temple for the Lord	2–4
		Dedicated the temple	5–7
		God appeared, agreeing to hear prayers offered in the temple as long as the people obeyed him.	7
		Built cities and conscripted slave labor; married Pharaoh's daughter	8
		Met the queen of Sheba and gave her great riches and wisdom; became wealthier and wiser than any king	9
		Mentioned	10–13, 30, 33, 35
Tobijah	Levite under King Jehoshaphat	Taught God's law to Judah	17

148

Uzziah	King of Judah, Amaziah's son	Followed the Lord at first, rebuilding towns and defeating enemies; struck with leprosy when he rebelled and entered the temple to burn incense	26
Zabad	Ammonite official of King Joash	Killed Joash after he turned from God	24
Zebadiah	Son of Ishmael, a Levite	Taught God's law to Judah Appointed over Jehoshaphat in matters concerning the king	17 19
Zechariah	Brother of King Jehoram	Murdered by Jehoram	21
Zechariah	Official of King Jehoshaphat	Taught God's law to Judah	17
Zechariah	Prophet during King Uzziah's reign	Taught Uzziah the fear of the Lord	26
Zechariah	Son of Jehoiada the priest	Killed by King Joash when he tried to turn him back to the Lord	24
Zedekiah	King of Judah, Jehoiachin's uncle	Made king after Jehoiachin was taken to Babylon; rebelled against God and Nebuchadnezzar; brought God's wrath against Judah and it was destroyed	36
Zedekiah	Son of Kenaanah, false prophet	Gave false prophecy of victory to Ahab	18
Zeduthun	Musician leader	Mentioned	5
Zerah	A Cushite	Defeated by Judah during King Abijah's reign	14
Zibeah	Mother of King Joash	Mentioned	24
Zicri	Warrior from Ephraim	Killed Maaseiah, Azrikam, and Elkanah	28

The Jewish Calendar

Each month of the Jewish calendar begins upon a new moon, which year to year occurs on different days of our Gregorian calendar months and rarely on the first day of a month. Thus, the relationship of Jewish calendar months to our Gregorian calendar months varies year to year.

In addition to the Levitical festivals below, there are twelve new moon festivals, and every Sabbath is a day of complete rest.

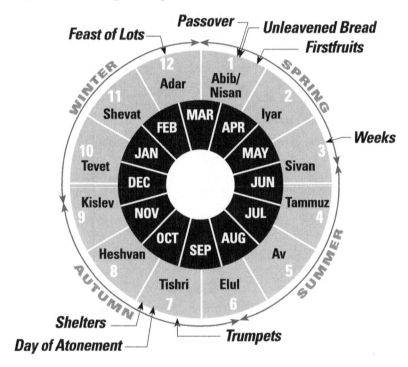

Subject Index

The subject begins at the cited verse. Second Chronicles is in italics.

Ark of the covenant	6:31; 13:3, 12; 15:1, 25; 16:1; 17:1; 22:19; 28:2, 18; *1:4; 5:2; 6:11, 41; 8:11; 35:3*
Blessing from	13:14
Death from touching	13:9
Rules for carrying	15:2, 13, 26; *5:4; 35:3*
Birthright	5:1
Covenants	11:3; 16:15; *15:12; 16:3; 23:1, 16*
Fasting	*20:3*
Festivals, celebration of	*8:13; 30:5, 13; 31:3; 35:1, 16*
Genealogies, descendants of	
Aaron and the Levites	15:5
Abraham	1:27
Adam	1:1
Asher	7:30
Benjamin	7:6; 8:1
Caleb	2:42
David	3:1
Ephraim	7:20
Issachar	7:1
Jacob (Israel)	2:1
Judah	4:1
Levi	6:1
Manasseh	7:14
Naphtali	7:13
Reuben	5:1
Saul	9:35
Seir	1:38
Simeon	4:24
God	
Abandoning	*12:1; 13:10; 15:2; 21:10; 24:18; 28:6; 29:6; 34:25*
Above all gods	16:25; 17:20; *2:5; 33:13*
Angel of	21:15, 30; *32:21*
Anger of (wrath of)	13:10; *12:7; 19:2, 10; 24:18; 25:15; 28:9, 13; 29:8; 30:8; 32:21, 25; 33:6; 34:21; 36:16*
Anointed of	11:3; 14:8; 16:22; 29:22; *6:42*
Blessed	16:36; 29:10, 20; *2:12; 6:4; 9:8; 20:26; 31:8*
Blessing of	13:14; 17:27; *31:10*
Compassion of	*30:9; 36:15*
Covenant of/with	16:15; *6:14; 13:5; 21:7; 29:10; 34:31*
Creator	16:26; *2:12*
Deliverer	11:14; 14:11; 16:35; 17:8, 21; 18:6; 22:9; *14:12; 18:31; 20:15, 20, 24; 26:7; 32:8, 21*
Dwells in darkness (a cloud)	*5:13; 6:1*
Enthroned between cherubim	13:6
Establishes kingdoms	14:2; 17:7, 11, 24; 22:10; 28:4; *6:6; 7:18; 17:5*
Fear of	13:12; 16:30; *6:31; 19:7; 20:29*

The Festivals of the Lord[a]

A sacred convocation is held on the first day of each festival. The offerings are in addition to the regular daily offerings, Sabbath offerings, and new moon offerings (see Numbers 28:3–15).

	Spring Festivals				Fall Festivals		
English Name	**Passover**[c]	**Unleavened Bread**[c]	**Firstfruits**	**Weeks**[c] (Pentecost, Harvest)	**Trumpets**	**Day of Atonement**	**Shelters**[c] (a.k.a. Tabernacles, Booths, Ingathering)
Hebrew Name	Pesach	Hag Hamatzot	Bikkurim	Shavuot	Rosh Hashanah	Yom Kippur	Sukkot
Purpose	Remember God passed over the Israelites when, to free them, he killed the firstborn of Egypt.	Remember leaving Egypt.	Recognize God's goodness in providing a crop.	Celebrate the grain harvest and God's giving of the Ten Commandments.	Celebrate the beginning of the new year.	Mourn sin, afflict the soul, and seek atonement.	Remember the exodus and forty years of wandering.
Dates[b] **Hebrew**	Abib 14	Abib 15–21	Abib 16	50th day after Passover	Tishri 1	Tishri 10	Tishri 15
Gregorian	Late March to late April			Mid-May to mid-June		Mid-September to mid-October	
Number of Days	One day	Six or seven days	One day	One day	One day	One day	Seven days
Offerings and Practices	Burnt and sin offerings. Seder meal. Eat no leavened bread. Rest, no work.	Daily offerings by fire. Eat no leavened bread. Rest, no work on 1st and 7th days.	Wave offering of sheaf of firstfruits. Burnt, grain, and wine offerings. Rest, no work.	Burnt and sin offerings. Rest, no work.	Burnt and sin offerings. Trumpet blasts.[d] Rest, no work.	Burnt, grain, and drink offerings. A complete fast. Rest, no work.	Burnt and sin offerings. Live in shelters. Rejoicing.
Scripture References	Exodus 12:1–14 Leviticus 23:5 Numbers 9:9–14; 28:16 Deuteronomy 16:1–8	Exodus 12:15–20; 13:3–10; 23:14–15 Leviticus 23:6–8 Numbers 28:17–25 Deuteronomy 16:1–8	Leviticus 23:9–14	Exodus 23:16; 34:22, 26 Leviticus 23:15–21 Numbers 28:26–31 Deuteronomy 16:9–12	Leviticus 23:23–25	Leviticus 23:26–32	Leviticus 23:33–43 Deuteronomy 16:13–17

a In addition to the Sabbath. See Leviticus 23:3.

b Because the dates are set according to the Jewish calendar, which is controlled by the phases of the moon, the dates vary from year to year in the Gregorian (today's) calendar.

c Pilgrimage festivals, meaning that all Jewish men were to come to Jerusalem to celebrate the festival. Some people consider Passover and Unleavened Bread to be one long event because they are next to each other.

d Unless it is on the Sabbath, in which case there are no trumpet blasts.

154

Note on Dates of Events

The exact year in which any event in the Bible took place is speculative. Today's *anno Domini* dating system was not invented until about AD 1525, more than a thousand years after the last words of Scripture were written. Before adopting the *anno Domini* system, people kept track of years by the regnal system, tying events to the year of the reigning king, governor, or lesser official (e.g., "in the fifteenth year of Tiberias Caesar"). People simply were not concerned about exact dates.

Because the biblical records were not written with the idea of recording dates, the information is incomplete. While there are means of estimating the dates, they are all guesstimates. The dates we present fall within the generally accepted date ranges used by biblical scholars.

Translation Notes

Translation Type: The Readable Bible is a literal translation[a] in the sense that each original language word is expressed in English. However, sometimes a literal translation is unlikely to communicate the writer's thought to a modern audience. For instance, people unfamiliar with ancient culture probably do not understand that the term "kiss the Son" in Psalm 2:12 means to show him homage. So, where the literal translation might confuse or mislead today's reader, a thought-for-thought translation is presented and the literal translation is footnoted, or vice versa (unless the term is listed in "Nonliteral Words and Phrases Not Footnoted"). When an action verb is immediately followed by another action verb (e.g., "got up and went"), oftentimes only the second verb is expressed in the English text.

Added Words: Sometimes the author left out words that he knew his audience would have in their minds due to their familiarity with the context, culture, and language. Today English-speaking readers need those words added to the text. Thus, we supply them, as well as other explanatory words, in *italics*. Italicized additions are also made to clarify the text or avoid confusion for readers who (1) are not familiar with Scripture truths and the history of Israel and (2) might not recognize when figures of speech (e.g., hyperboles, metaphors) are being used.

Grammar: As is common in modern translations, the words are not always expressed in the grammatical form of the original text when that creates awkward English. Instead, the text is presented as we speak today. Occasionally, for clarity or ease of reading, we substitute a noun for a pronoun, or vice versa.

Hinneh: The Hebrew word *hinneh* calls attention to what follows. It indicates an emotional moment, brings focus upon a dialogue or a report, or expresses a person's reaction to a situation. While it is not directly translatable into English, "behold" is used in older translations, and "look" is used in more modern ones. The Readable Bible expresses it with a word or phrase such as "look," "notice," "pay attention," "believe me," "suddenly," and "was surprised to see." While it is common for modern translations to ignore the word, The Readable Bible almost always renders it.

Uncertain Translation: Many Hebrew words have several meanings. If an equally viable alternate term or phrase would give the text a significantly different sense or feel than the one given by the word we render, we provide the alternate in a notation.

Weights and Measures: Current equivalents are presented in rounded, easy-to-read amounts. The literal text is footnoted. The equivalents are uncertain because ancient measures varied by time and place, and archaeological information is incomplete. Coinage[b] can be expressed somewhat accurately in weight, but it is more difficult to translate its value into terms that relate accurately to today. The exact amount does not appear to be crucial to the meaning of any passage.

---

a   The Old Testament translation is based primarily upon the Biblia Hebraica Stuttgartensia (BHS), 5th edition. Some passages are modified due to questionable BHS text and/or more recent manuscript discoveries. Such modifications draw from the Septuagint, Dead Sea Scrolls, Samaritan Pentateuch, Targums, and Syriac text. The Masoretic text is noted, as is the source of the modification.

b   Until the first government-issued coinage was made in about 600 BC, coinage was simply pieces of metal used as a medium of exchange.

Format and Presentation Notes

The Readable Bible presents text that is as readable as any other twenty-first-century nonfiction work. Here are a few of the ways that is accomplished.

Callouts, Headings, Bold Type: These features help keep you oriented and aid information searches. Callout boxes and headings that are not part of sentences are not part of the inspired text. The words in boldface are not more important than any other words of the text.

Capitalization: Personal pronouns that refer to God are not capitalized unless necessary for clarity (as there is no such distinction in the original manuscripts). The term "spirit" is capitalized when it refers to God.

Contractions: Rather than adhere to modern literature standards such as MLA style or *Chicago Manual of Style*, the translation varies language style according to context. Contractions are used as they might normally be used by today's writers and speakers (i.e., inconsistently, not in every possible place but in many). This results in a more natural text that improves readability yet does not affect meaning.

Lists: Items in a series are sometimes presented in list format. These should be read down the first column and then down the next column.

Nonliteral Text: Words and phrases not translated literally and appearing more than three times in a book are not footnoted. Instead, the literal translation is provided in the "Nonliteral Words and Phrases Not Footnoted" table in the back of the book.

Quote Marks: Ancient writings used "said" to indicate a direct quotation. Today we use quotation marks for the same purpose. Thus, when the manuscript text reads, "The Lᴏʀᴅ spoke to Moses, saying, '[quote].' " The Readable Bible reads, "The Lᴏʀᴅ said to Moses, '[quote].' "

Slashes: The slash between words in a footnote represents "or" or "and/or."

Tables: Tables are used for object specifications, genealogies, census and other numerical data, and some lists. Table headings list the verses that are rendered solely in that table. This list does not include verses referenced in the table that are fully rendered in their normal location outside the table. Quantities in italics are calculated, not in the Hebrew text.

Verse numbers preceding table text refer to the following text until the next number. At times a verse number follows table text and applies to the text before and after it until the next entry with a verse number beside it.

Text Location: Some text has been moved to increase readability and clarity, to conform with modern paragraph construction practice, or to group like information in a single location. When text is moved to a different page, its chapter and verse(s) are noted in its new location, and its new location is noted in its original location. On occasion, adjacent verses are grouped together when sentences and phrases have been rearranged to conform to English composition norms.

Transliteration: When a transliterated proper noun first appears in the text, if its English translation adds clarity or meaning to the text, it is provided within parentheses like this: "Nod (*i.e.*, Wandering)."

Nonliteral Words and Phrases Not Footnoted

The Readable Bible oftentimes renders the word "said" as an equivalent word that expresses the inner dialogue and/or feeling and/or emotion with which the words were spoken (e.g., announced, asked, answered, called to/out, cautioned, claimed, complained, confirmed, continued, declared, directed, wondered).

We follow the normal English Bible translation practice of inserting words that are not in the Hebrew text at the start of a sentence to facilitate smooth reading (e.g., "so," "now," "then," "when," "rather"). Thus, "then" does not mean an event directly followed a preceding event, though it might have. The reader must use their own judgment based on context.

When a place-name occurs without part of its normal English title, we add the title (e.g., "Jordan" becomes "Jordan River"; "Negev" becomes "Negev Desert").

The literal translation of the dynamic expressions below are not footnoted when the dynamic translation occurs three or more times. Not all occurrences of the literal expressions below are translated dynamically.

Dynamic Translation (Nonliteral)	Literal Translation
Army	People ("Army" is used in military contexts.)
Country	Land of [Country]
Family	House, father's house
Founder of	Father of
Home, to their	House/tent, to their

Israelites
  All the Israelites
	People of Israel
	  All Israel

Palace	House of the king
People of [city]	The dwellers of/in [city]
Replied	Replied to [name or description] E.g., "replied to Nathan"; "replied to the people"
Sent messengers	Sent
Subjects	Servants
Temple	House
Trading ships	Ships to Tarshish
Warrior	Men of war, mighty man, mighty man of valor

If you enjoyed this book, will you consider sharing the message with others?

Let us know your thoughts. You can let the author know by visiting or sharing a photo of the cover on our social media pages or leaving a review at a retailer's site. All of it helps us get the message out!

Email: info@ironstreammmedia.com

   @ironstreammedia

Iron Stream, Iron Stream Fiction, Iron Stream Kids, Brookstone Publishing Group, and Life Bible Study are imprints of Iron Stream Media, which derives its name from Proverbs 27:17, "As iron sharpens iron, so one person sharpens another." This sharpening describes the process of discipleship, one to another. With this in mind, Iron Stream Media provides a variety of solutions for churches, ministry leaders, and nonprofits ranging from in-depth Bible study curriculum and Christian book publishing to custom publishing and consultative services.

For more information on ISM and its imprints, please visit IronStreamMedia.com

Printed in Great Britain
by Amazon

46097414R00099